LIVING WITHOUT LIMITATIONS

VISION QUEST

Compiled by: Anita Sechesky

LWL PUBLISHING HOUSE

Brampton, Canada

CONTENTS

LEGAL DISCLAIMER

FOREWORD

Growing up, I fondly recall my mother always stating that I was "a fighter for the underdog." But let me start at the very beginning…

Before birth, when I was swimming in my mom's belly as a tiny, peanut-sized fetus, I would glide inside her uterus, stopping frequently to sport jazz hands and to do a couple of fancy turns. Yes, my soul always knew I was destined to grace stages across the world. I already had the vision of my life's purpose, as so many of us do, from conception.

At a young age, I had to accept that life would be different for me. I had congestive heart failure and the whole left side of my body was structurally damaged. Throughout my childhood, there were ongoing surgeries and hospital stays. But, I had a vision and nothing was going to stand in my way.

I became a fighter – someone who would push the boundaries and keep going until I reached my destination. It didn't matter that I still had physical limitations.

I was the underdog who never veered from my vision and would often stand up for other devoted souls going against the grain. Throughout my life, I've also faced difficulties fitting in and trying to be understood by my peers. However, nothing could stop me, even with my health challenges because I had no choice but to acknowledge them, as they are part of my physical DNA. Your spiritual DNA connects you on your journey with who you are and where you're meant to travel.

So what really is Vision?

True vision is something deep inside our souls that is undeniable, relentlessly driving us forward when we have the gumption to say yes to it *(while many in our circle may think we have lost our marbles!)*. It is something that starts as little pinches and grows into a perpetual nagging that cannot be denied until it has been satisfied with our taste for accomplishment and success.

Life will always give you choices and what direction you go in will determine the outcome you are looking for. We all have a divine vision that is only achieved when we are willing to boldly step up and laser focus onto it. It's that single-minded fierceness that opens the gates to seeing it through to completion brilliantly.

Imagine it this way: You know your destiny is on the other side of the ocean. You decide to send a message in a bottle to say, "Here I come." You pull out the empty bottle of last night's Chardonnay. You start writing out the vision and doubt creeps in – "Can I really do this? Maybe I should ask for less. Maybe I need to start small. Is this really want I want? Hmmm... perhaps I will send out a few notes so I have options."

The bottle is thrown into the ocean, rides on the back of a whale and is tossed onto the shore of this brave new land. When the bottle is opened, there is so much "noise" in there from all the messages that the receiver has no idea what the messenger is trying to say. It's all muddled. Nothing happens.

Clarity and relentless commitment can be scary, but they can also be exhilarating. They are the gateways to crossing the ocean successfully. I have seen it countless times in my own life. Every opportunity that I was willing to be uncomfortable with, despite being so far outside my platform, and truly speak exactly what I wanted, my life experiences deepened in ways that were profoundly beautiful. For years now, despite all my health challenges, I have been gracing stages across the world and training my courageous clients on how they too can step onto their own stage and make an impact in their field of expertise.

As you read through this compilation, you will see that our authors had to dig deep within themselves to find their direction in life. It takes courage to be willing to commit to a single, laser-focused vision without having "proof" that it could actually happen. You will find yourself being inspired over and over to create your vision, dive into the unknown, and play with new possibilities.

You are the visionary of your life. Breathe... you've got this!

Love Cindy

Cindy Ashton, Award Winning Stage & Presence Coach, Professional Speaker, Singer and Entertainer

Cindy is an award-winning global leader, stage and presence coach and professional speaker / singer / entertainer. She has received awards from both President Obama & the Queen of England for her lifetime of volunteerism and has appeared in multiple media including on the front page of the lifestyle section of the Times.

Born with a 20% chance of living, heart failure and structural damage, Cindy has undergone multiple heart surgeries and has lived with lifelong chronic illness. Despite it all, she has gone on to build a successful business, be highly regarded as an expert in her field and become masterful on stage as both a speaker and performer. She models how to live outside the lines with grace, inspiring to all who cross her path.

Connect with Cindy at www.YourPersuasiveVoice.com and www.CindyAshton.com

ACKNOWLEDGEMENTS

It is with heartfelt appreciation and gratitude that I take this time to acknowledge the people who have stood by, supported, and loved me for exactly who I am. Through all things I am blessed because of the peace of God and the blanket of love that continually surrounds me and lifts me up when I may be feeling down.

Thank you Stephen, the love of my life for believing in me and my desire to always strive for greater purpose in all that I do. Your unconditional love, support and friendship have inspired me on this journey. Thank you for being who you are to me and our boys.

To my eldest son Nathaniel: Thank you for being such an amazing son, I love you more and more each day. You inspire me and make me so proud to be your mother. You are an intelligent, kind and loving individual. I adore your sense of humor and appreciate all the special gifts God has blessed you with to appreciate knowledge and seek wisdom in all your ways. Always remember what an amazing gift from God you are, to not only your family, but also to those around you. Never give up on your dreams and ambitions. You were a success from the day you were born. You are perfect to me. I will always believe in you. Love Mom.

To Sammy: Thank you, my darling son for the joy that you bring to Mommy. I love your curiosity as a child, always fixing and taking things apart. You have the mind of a genius with so much potential. The world is unfolding before your very eyes. You never cease to amaze me with your growing wisdom and skills. God has great plans for you. You are perfect to me. Success is in every step that you take. I'm so proud to call you "My little darling." I will always believe in you. Love Mommy.

To my beautiful Mother Jean Seergobin: Thank you mom for always encouraging me to see the beauty in the world around me and inspiring me to never give up. You are my best friend mom and I love you so much with all my heart. It is because of you that I have learned gentleness and compassion in this life. Thank you Mom. To my loving Father, Jetty Seergobin: Thank you Dad for showing me how to never be discouraged in life but to carry on despite whatever circumstances I may be facing. You have been my source of inspiration and hope because of the values you taught me from such a young age. Mom and Dad, I love you both so much, because of your unconditional and unfailing love for me. I have been encouraged, impassioned, motivated and blessed because of your acceptance of me as your child. I have not been perfect, I have not always done what you expected of me, I have not always taken your advice, but yet you have never let me down. In fact, you have always welcomed me with open arms and shown me what unconditional love really is. In a world full of hate, criticism, and jealousy, Mom and Dad you have both guided me to be a better person. I have gone through many trials, tribulations, and discouragements in my life and it is because of your constant love and belief in me with the grace of God that I have overcome. I am a better person today because of you both. I am ever so thankful for your love and prayers over my life from the time I was conceived and I am blessed. I speak blessings of health, wholeness, happiness, and long life over you both. May the grace of God's divine love and protection be around you always. I love you Mom and Dad.

To my brother Trevor Seergobin: Thank you for your friendship, and encouragement. I am very blessed because you are my brother.

For all of the people who have been part of my life and supported my dreams and ambitions, thank you for being the wonderful friends, colleagues, and family that you are to me. I love and appreciate each one of you. I am grateful to every individual who has contributed to the woman that I am today. It is because of your unconditional love towards me that I am inspired and encouraged to dream and do more for others. I have grown emotionally strong through my own painful experiences so that I can allow others to do the same. There were many friendships that have come along side for a season and I acknowledge and value you for sharing that moment of your life with me. I have not forgotten. You are in a special place within my heart.

Once again I would like to give an unusual appreciation to those who have caused me heartache, disappointments, and pain. You were the lessons that I needed at that particular time in my life so that I can be a better person today. Because of you, I never gave up in life. It was the hardships that you put me through which made me strive harder to believe in the unconditional love that is lacking in this world. Two wrongs never make a right. I forgive. Love does cover a multitude of sins.

I Peter 4:8

DEDICATION

This book is dedicated to all the people, young or old, who have experienced criticism and harsh experiences which have left them feeling spiritually broken or damaged. We are all beautiful people of the earth and together we can inspire one another to reach higher and heal more. I empower you to believe once again in the power of you. There was a time in my life I had no one to lift me up and encourage me, but my faith. My world felt so small. Now because of my bigger vision to step outside of what I knew, I'm able to see more, and I tell you...with God nothing is impossible. The world is waiting for your vision. And if no one still believes in you, I do!

Life always gets better, but first, one must believe.

Anita Sechesky

INTRODUCTION

When I envisioned the completion of this book, I had a goal for it to have specific facets that would leave the impression that nothing is impossible, in every sense of the word. We have all heard this said so many times and in many different ways, that I believe it can be overused. It feels as if it's being regurgitated in such a way that people tend to lose hope far too quickly, and in doing so lose sight of their own goals and ambitions in life.

The concept for this book, my third in the *Living Without Limitations* series, is not meant to create fictional idealisms but to actually generate solid foundations of hope and empowerment for the reader.

As a Registered Nurse, Certified Professional Coach, Author, and Publisher, it is part of my work ethics to always have several plans in motion at any given time. I realize this is not how the average person may manage their everyday life, but it's an actuality that's worked effectively for me before I became an R.N. more than ten years ago. I had already integrated this lifestyle when I was a new mom with a five-month-old baby and attending a full-time nursing program.

I had made a promise to myself that I would become a Registered Nurse. It was a dream that I carried within my heart since I was in Grade Four, where I received a scholastic report determining what my "Best" and ideal career choices would be. Well, I must have been very upset by receiving a "Future Career" score that determined my most ideal qualities fit being a hairdresser. So much so that I promised myself, walking home on that warm spring day, to never give up until I achieved my goal – R.N. Now, make no mistake. I also loved cutting hair and I did manage to give my dolls quite the styles with food coloring to be creative and fun. My friends had even volunteered for these experiences and it was a risk they were willing to take, even if it meant wearing a barrette on one side of their heads for the next several months. That's when you know you've got friends that believe in you no matter what!

Growing up, I didn't always have the support from individuals I would have liked to. You see, for some reason, I was perceived as "different" and for that, I always knew when I was being talked about. My internal radar was on high alert at all times. Have you ever been in a room and all you hear is a buzz? You look around and you see the faces, but you don't care to know their names because the sound of your radar buzzing has got you poised and in protection mode. Your senses have picked up on the indifference of others. Well that's the kind of buzz I am talking about – you can feel that they already have their own perceptions about you whether they know you or not. It doesn't matter what they are chit-chatting about, you know it isn't good because the energy you are picking up is literally pushing you out of the room. I had lived with that for so many years. I first noticed it when I was very young and starting school in Canada after emigrating from Guyana, South America. My outward appearance made me stand out quite beautifully, in my opinion. I was glowing with sun-kissed skin and pierced ears at the sweet age of four. I was the talk of the gym class; the other girls would touch my skin to see how it felt and asked what language I spoke even though they understood what I said. You see, my accent was West Indian and it had a special flair that was sometimes difficult to decipher for the average Northerner. My ears were also pierced and I had pretty gold earrings, something that Canadian girls at that time did not get until they were older, and it was fascinating to my new peers.

The reason I'm sharing these details with you is that this was the beginning of what helped to mold me into who I am today. I'm so grateful for the intolerable differences and uncomfortable experiences I have walked through. They have helped to prepare me for the many ordeals I have experienced in life.

Remember that "buzzing" I had mentioned earlier that I frequently heard when entering places or events? Well, I don't hear it anymore. I have discovered how to master the moments in my life so that I'm not affected by the negativity and hate that is around me any longer. In fact, I got so annoyed at my allowing it to drown out any good that was waiting for me that I chose to let go of the destructive behaviors, attitudes, and influences of others. This was my secret that allowed me to boldly step into the life I wanted for myself.

As this amazing compilation came together within these past few months, it was evident that the dream was coming into alignment. Although it did have a few adjustments along the way, the final outcome has far surpassed my greatest expectations. You see, initially I had only perceived having ten unique and empowered individuals who were confident of themselves stepping into something that would either enhance what they already represent or allow them an opportunity to have a far greater outreach by embracing this opportunity to share their story of evolving and stepping into the goals that they had to birth into the world.

Also, part of my original strategy was to invite individuals who attended my Living Without Limitations Conferences in Brampton and Thunder Bay, Ontario this past year. I actually achieved this goal quite quickly and ended up having my two International Speakers from the U.K., both of whom had attended the Inaugural Launch of our Conference series, join Vision Quest right away. Moving forward, I felt an incompletion in the configuration of the book, so I allowed for smaller yet compelling chapters from additional individuals who inquired if I was still accepting contributors. Following that, I was inspired to add Vision Tips throughout the book. These are very focused topics for the reader, no story lines or in-depth experiences shared. Just right to the point information, advice, and empowerment for everyone.

Living Without Limitations – Vision Quest is a book that will take you into the lives of some very accomplished individuals who have devoted themselves to empowering others to step into their greatest roles. My intention is to give you inspiration irregardless of who you are. I want to show you that we all have to start somewhere. It doesn't matter who has never believed in you before, WE believe in you. Life won't get better because you read this amazing book; it gets better by the steps you take after you READ it and how you apply the resources that life presents you with. Can you take your career and life goals to the next level? Of course you can, but, "Do you believe?" is the real question you should be asking yourself. Every single person that has ever accomplished anything in life, has made the very same decision. When were they going to start? So many times we tell ourselves we'll get to something, and so many times that moment never happens because we don't stick to our plan, our "vision" and follow through. We have no one to blame but ourselves. Society may cause us to believe otherwise in subtle forms. "Well, I didn't have a cheering squad behind me". "They never gave me a chance". Or how about, "I never knew I could do it because I wasn't confident of myself and I'm afraid of failing again." So many reasons to give up and so many dreams dying so easily. What's your excuse? Did you have a rough life? Lack of finances? Maybe not motivated enough? You see my friend, we all have the same opportunities if we really look closely. Life is not guaranteed to be easy for anyone, and if it appears effortless for some, there's a good chance you don't know the troubles that person has faced. Not all limitations and road blocks in life are visible to the human eye.

The reason this book is something you want to keep close to you isn't because it's an inspirational book. We're being real and telling you that it can be done. Not everyone will be a billionaire in their lifetime, and not everyone wants to be. Some people just want to be debt free and established. Others want the chance to make a difference right where they are. You see, our world has many levels and meanings of success. This is a good thing because it means there are more opportunities for everyone and less competition. Life should never be a competition unless you're running in a race because the energy you surround yourself with is desperation – emitting the frequency and energy of lack. These are definitely not what success is attracted to.

By reading the chapters in this book, you will find your perceptions shifting. Success stories all have a history; this is what makes them so powerful. The very fact that you're reading this book is the first evidence of that. You made a decision to make this year the best year possible of your life. You've invested in your growth and self-empowerment by accepting to be open-minded and ready for change in whichever way is necessary to move forward. Congratulations!

Now that I have shared the conceptions of this incredible book, I want to also say that every dream has flexibility and room to stretch and grow. As you continue reading, I'll be sharing more about what that really means and why I so strongly believe far too many individuals sabotage their own successes in life because of this internal limitation.

I would like to introduce you to my courageous co-authors who have discovered their own ways to master their life moments and accomplish their Vision Quests.

As you can see I have given you proof that goals do change and we should allow ourselves the freedom to perfect it. Don't be hard on yourself because we're living in a time where anything is possible. Men have already walked on the moon and now there is evidence that life is habitable elsewhere. Nothing is impossible if you believe.

What's your Vision Quest? Let's take this journey together.

Anita Sechesky is a Publisher, Registered Nurse, Certified Professional Coach, NLP and LOA Wealth Practitioner, Best-Seller Consultant, multiple International Best-Selling Author, as well as Workshop Facilitator and Conference Host. She is the Founder and CEO of Anita Sechesky - Living Without Limitations Inc. and the Founder and Publisher of LWL PUBLISHING HOUSE. Anita was born in Guyana, South America and moved to Canada when she was four-years-old. She has assisted many people breaking through their own limiting beliefs in life and business. Anita has four Best-Selling books, three of which were anthologies consisting of seventy-five International co-authors. Anita launched her first solo book *"Absolutely You – Overcome False Limitations and Reach Your Full Potential"* in November 2014. As a Best-Seller Publisher, Anita helps people to put their positive perspectives into print.

To begin the exciting journey as a VIP Compiler™ with Anita on your own anthology book, or to learn more about becoming a co-author with LWL PUBLISHING HOUSE in one of our many anthologies, please visit our Facebook page "LWL PUBLISHING HOUSE", visit our website: www.lwlpublishinghouse.com, or email: lwlclienthelp@gmail.com. For more details, please see the Conclusion at the end of this book, on page 139.

ESTABLISHING

THE

VISION

CHAPTER I   Anita Sechesky

Establishing The Vision

How many times have you felt a desire to start something and yet never seemed to get it done? I would like to take this opportunity to help you understand what a Vision really is. After all, if you have no clue, how in the world can you be expected to produce something that has no validity or reference point?

Life sometimes has a way of getting us caught up in so many things that we put our own desires aside because we find ourselves a person of circumstances. We basically allow life to happen to us, as we feel we have no control with our choices. This can be the case for many people, so don't feel bad – understanding is the beginning of all wisdom.

Here are a few points that I feel are critical to establishing the Vision in your own life.

I. Discover what your "true north" is and use it as a guidance point of reference in everything you do moving forward in life. This will help with all decision-making along the way. By discovering what your goal or true north is in life, you'll be able to steer clear from things that will only take you further away from your ultimate goals. Not everyone understands the significance of this. It can be misconstrued that if you don't support others, you're not a nice person. In fact, in my opinion it's better to allow others the freedom to be who they are and follow their own paths in life. If you care about that individual and you do not resonate with their goals or ambitions in life, you're honoring them by allowing others who are in alignment of those individual's goals to come along side and authentically resonate with their vision. As for yourself, using a focal point will always bring you back to safety, figuratively speaking, and also eliminate unnecessary heartaches and disappointments. Why should you feel bad for not accomplishing something you don't have your heart fully committed to anyways?

2. Your Vision must be something that you can experience on an intimate level, meaning your senses come alive because your adrenaline is pumping and the very thought of achieving it makes your heart beat faster with anticipation and delight! Do you remember what it feels like to fall in love? Well that pretty much summarizes what the emotional connection to one's vision must be for it to ever have a chance to become a serious commitment. As you continue to express your deep love for your vision, the bond will begin to strengthen and you will finally be able to release the things that have kept you stuck and in the same cycle for too long. After all, isn't that the reason your vison presented itself in the first place? Sometime ago, you actually attracted your vision because of your internal desires. It has now shown up in your life to show you your potential and give you the opportunity to live authentically. This is where it can also become messy, just like a relationship that has no real substance and connection. If you are not deeply committed and connected, the vision will perish and not go any further as there's no solid foundation to grow from.

3. How much have you fallen in love with your vision? Believe it or not, if you don't love your vision, why should anyone else? Are you talking about it with everyone? Why aren't you proud to share it with your friends? I find this quite concerning when someone comes to me and says they have a vision, yet I cannot see evidence of it, so that makes me question the commitment. I look at a vision as if it were a child that needed nurturing. From the time it was conceived, it needs to be cared for and protected in such a way that it can grow strong and healthy. Mothers can relate very easily to this concept so for the gentlemen reading this part, try to envision yourself as the Father of your vision. Ultimately the parent must provide and care for this precious vision so it can becomes everything it was intended to be. As you strengthen it from your spiritual womb, it grows its legs to stand on and its arms to reach out and touch others. It becomes unique with your resemblance and takes on a life of its own. Your vision should become something bigger than you are, and a part of your identity even after its birth. By giving it the association of who you are, it's empowered to take on a life of its own, fulfilling the destiny it was created for.

4. Every vision must have an expected date of birth. If this is not established, there is no clear gestation period and it remains questionable if it will ever manifest. People around will wonder if you miscarried your vision and may see that you never gave the chance it really deserved. You may live with the guilt of not allowing that vision to take life and with this burden of loss it can become unbearable, especially if it really was in alignment with your true north destiny. Therefore, it is essential to determine a realistic

timeframe for your vison to be birthed. Consider the things in your life and accept that in order for success to take place, it will mean a commitment like no other. That's what sets it apart from your other goals and ambitions in life. This is how important your vision is. If you continue being involved with many things that take up your time and creative energy, you will not have the realistic opportunity to allow your vision the chance it needs. This is a significant reason why so many visions are miscarried early on and never given the opportunity to develop.

CHAPTER 2   Candace Hawkshaw

Light Up The Darkness

I had the best life growing up on a farm. I fell in love at an early age, married at eighteen, and began having children. By the time I was twenty-four, I had three beautiful daughters, two of whom were twins. My life looked much like everyone else's; raising children, working, and having vacations. I was busy taking care of everyone else, and I was happy.

Over time I began to lose pieces of myself. It hit me hard one night when we received a call that our teenage daughter was hospitalized with alcohol poisoning. I told my husband I wanted to stay with her that night, but he wouldn't allow it. As a mother, I felt I had abandoned my child in ICU. Leaving her bedside revealed a part of me that I didn't like. I believed that I had given away my power to keep the peace with my husband. It was a devastating truth. My marriage fell apart not long after that. I felt I was losing myself and my power of choice. I began to question, "Who was I, really?"

Other intimate relationships revealed to me that I was always drawn to men who I thought I could fix. I ended up losing myself, but in truth I had never really known who I was. I have experienced bankruptcy; started over again more than once. At one point I begged to be taken from this world. The answer I got was, "It's not your time yet, and you have work to do." I didn't know what that meant until a few months later. I turned the darkness into light. I became certified in Reiki. When I walked out of that class, I felt like my eyes were wide open and a new life was about to begin. I became a Reiki Master. My family and friends couldn't believe how I lit up, how my eyes and whole aura were different. I felt alive and such a power of love. I set up my own practice. Clients said my sessions were wonderful. The healing I was channeling for them began to heal me. It revealed what had been happening to me for so long. I finally understood that the sadness, anger, and depression were coming from other sources. It was freeing to understand this and to not own what wasn't really mine. I was an empath and was picking up on energies around me. My business grew and I was taking the healing work to different spas. The income, however, wasn't enough to sustain me, so I returned to the business world.

Corporate life is easy for me in some ways as I am an organized, creative, and an understanding manager. However, I got caught up in that life again, and stopped doing healings on myself and others. I felt like my light was extinguishing because I was in an environment filled with manipulation, gossip, and drama. I didn't fit in. I was also scheduled to have major surgery which, I believe, was the push from the Universe to make me stop long enough to re-evaluate my life.

During my recovery, I would sit in the backyard the blue jays would come very close to me. Animals bring messages and I was curious. Blue jays come to tell us that it is time to step into our truth, and find the resources within to make changes. Recognition dawned on me; I had given away my power in so many ways. I was lying to myself in every sense; from the job I had, to the relationship I was in, and the way I had let my health and spirituality take a backseat. Courageously, I left the job and the relationship to move back to my home town. Stepping out of fear and taking responsibility for my life, I opened a wellness business and have never looked back. It's been a gift that has taught me who I am and how much I love the work I am called to. I finally love myself.

I continue to manifest truth in my life. Over the next five years I envision travelling and teaching Reiki around the globe. I am already working towards hosting international retreats to assist people in lighting up their own darkness; to recognize and take back their own power.

Within ten years I want to own a log cabin in the forest, with water running through the property and wildlife everywhere. I will continue to travel internationally and teach Reiki with advanced forms of healing as the world continues to wake up. We are all magic and powerful. I am a facilitator for the new paradigm. We cannot survive with old, outmoded ways of thinking and being. It is time to light up the darkness.

Candace Hawkshaw is a Certified Reiki Master Teacher, Healer, Channel, Psychic, Soul Realignment Practitioner, and a sought after guide. She radiates love and kindness and holds a sacred space for healing without judgement. Candace has a strong connection with Mother Earth and lives a lifestyle based on the principles of Reiki that have changed her life. She has learned an evolved Reiki called Holy Fire. Her channeled wisdom comes through strongly when she speaks. She has grown and continually evolves. Candace uses her own experiences and wisdom to assist others on their journey. She teaches Holy Fire Reiki, transformation programs, and workshops.

www.soaringspirit.ca
https://www.pinterest.com/soaringspir0056

How To Have A Single Parent's Vision

My journey into parenthood wasn't one that turned out quite how I envisioned it. I was a single parent three times: at the ages of nineteen, twenty-four, and thirty-six. I then became a Grandmother in my 40's and 50's. I have been on a very long journey, but one I would not change for it has afforded me wisdom, experience, and personal growth.

I won't bore you with the details of the challenges and what didn't work, but rather would like to draw reference to what I found was successful for myself.

One point of reference I would like to make is to ensure that you maintain a sense of personal identity in terms of your own goals and aspirations. Draw reference to the skills that you will acquire as you grow alongside your children. These skills are termed transferrable skills, which you can use propel and motivate yourself. Nobody anticipates being placed in the position of raising a child or an entire family alone. If you ever find yourself in such a situation, the key objective is to allow yourself to become resourceful and tap into all of the skills you never knew you had. Believe me when I say this – you will have many.

Another great tip is to learn to channel yourself particularly in the area of creativeness. Be original and creative, take pictures, draw, start a blog, or write a journal. Imaginatively expressing yourself is a great form of interpretation. Once you find an outlet for your expression you are well on you way there.

My tips for juggling Parenthood are as follows:

• Acknowledge that you are already successful. Raising a child alone is one of the biggest challenges you will face.
• Tap into your skills and your resourcefulness.
• Keep a sense of focus always.
• Never lose your dream.
• Always follow your inner passion. It's been speaking to you throughout your life.
• Follow your intuition (inner voice).
• Recognize that obstacles exist; they do not have to prevent you from moving forward.
• Feel proud of your accomplishments, however small and reward yourself.

- Use setbacks to motivate yourself for personal growth.
- Use resources such as "To Do" lists, vision boards, and smart action planning.
- Break goals down into short term, medium term, and long term goals.
- Learn to laugh at yourself. Humility helps.
- Enjoy the journey
- Reach out and ask for help. Accept help if it is offered or given.
- Be grateful and show gratitude.
- Do not be afraid to take risks.
- Get creative and be creative.
- Get expressive and be expressive.
- Learn to dance with Life.
- Learn to dream.
- Embrace your success.

CHAPTER 3   Janette Burke

Don't Stop Believing!

Memories light the corners of my mind. Misty water color memories of the way things were. Scattered pictures of the smiles we left behind...smiles we gave to one another for the way we were.

There I was, all of three-years-old, clinging to my make-shift skipping rope microphone, as I sang my heart out in the middle of our living room for my parents and their friends.

"She sure loves the spotlight." "Yes, she gets that from me and my family," said my mother. "And she can sort of carry a tune! Not as good as that famous female singer yet. But there's always hope, with a little practice."

Now you have to realize that well-known female entertainers were like Goddesses in my home, not just because of their incredible talent and fame, but because they were Jewish Women who made it, big.

In this very moment, I, a Jewish girl living in small town Ontario with very few friends and ever fewer outlets, came to life. Somewhat isolated and misunderstood, I was a very outgoing and jovial child with a flair for mischief, fashion, and fun — continuously criticized for being independent, rebellious, and non-conforming.

Many tried to change me and failed. Performing was the arena I needed — the place that I could be my true self. It took all the ignorant stereo-types, name calling, finger-pointing, shaming, pain and suffering of being Jewish, slightly chubby (depending on what diet I was currently on) and of being deemed "different" away — making me feel whole inside. So naturally, I wanted more of it.

In fact, as I continued to grow, I told my parents several times over that "I was meant to be living in Beverly Hills amongst my people." People I believed would accept and respect me. I actually planned to move there, land a role on one of the most popular Soap Opera, then work my way up to TV & movies. And win an Oscar.

But my parents had other ideas.

In typical Jewish parent fashion, they came at me with a slew of dream-killing questions "You can't just pick-up and move to Hollywood. You're a Canadian without a green card. You have no real talent or training as an actress or a singer, no agent, and no connections. You are also on the short and sometimes stout side," and the excuses went on. I would holler back "Size and shape don't determine whether a person can sing, dance, and act. I can do it and I will!"

"You and a million other people!" they shouted. "Do you know what your chances of making it are? We don't need a starving artist to support." "You want to make waiting tables your living? How and where will you live? We have more in-store for you," they went on.

"We love you and want only the very best for you. So you will go to University, get educated, find yourself a nice guy from a good family - perhaps a doctor, lawyer, or accountant," my mother would add, "to marry, settle-down, and have children with." "And if he's smart and ambitious with some sales sense, Daddy will teach him to take over the business. Or maybe you can." As if I wanted to!

"We don't mind if you want to sing, dance and act on the side for some enjoyment. But thank God you were also born with a brain and a mouth. Stop with the star-struck already, apply yourself and focus on what really matters, Janette." In other words, settle for second best.

"If you like acting, why not become a lawyer, act in the courtroom and get paid handsomely for it?" my mother would suggest. "You love people, asking questions, hearing their stories, are a little go-getter, can sell snow to an Eskimo and have the gift of the gab," she would continue, "I think law or following in the foot-steps of another admired Jewess will turn out to be your destiny."

With my real dreams put on hold, I began seeking alternative channels in which to release my creativity.

First was working in my father's men's clothing stores, selling and learning the art of promotional marketing. It was the Christmas Season and the best day ever! Not only did I get to go to work with my dad "The Pro", I got to interact with the customers, ask key questions, determine their needs and solve them. Within three hours of being on the floor (where I was told to stay in the front with the underwear and other small stuff), I became bored. As luck would have it, my father and staff were busy tending to other customers and didn't notice me approaching "the nice lady" that just arrived.

I greeted her warmly and asked how I could help. Twenty minutes later, I earned my first commission on the suit, matching shirt, tie, puff and socks she purchased for her husband!

Waiting on customers remained a joy. But my *imaginative* side needed further feeding.

By the time I was fifteen, I was alongside my mother, *The PR Queen*, creating sales copy, slogans, print, radio & television ads, customer incentives & rewards, fashion shows, and special events that proved to be more "My Thing." But to survive living in Belleville and fulfilling my parent's expectations, I still needed other outlets to throw myself into.

Keeping active and busy is something I've always loved. I maintained my academics and high grades in both regular school and Hebrew school that I attended three times a week plus Sunday mornings until the time of my Bat Mitzvah at age twelve.

Other interests and activities that took up the rest of my time included: hanging with my friends, experiencing other cultures, escaping as often as possible to Kingston, Toronto, Montreal, Florida and New York on family vacations and buying adventures, winning a bursary to live with a French-Canadian Family and spend a summer living outside of Quebec City learning to speak French, continuing to work in my Dad's store, participating in community theatre, piano, playing the flute in my high school band, volunteering, summer school (which I took to graduate early) and creating a Fashion Show for my High School with acted-out themes and sponsors that generated $1,500 in one night.

When I was eighteen, I headed straight for The University of Western Ontario where I spent three glorious years earning a Bachelor's of Social Science degree in Political Science and Economics followed by another year at York University where I obtained my Honors Equivalency in Social and Classical Studies.

In between my six essay-writing and other courses, I served as a Social Director for The Jewish Student's Union/Hillel and Classical Studies Student's Federation.

Here again, I was given the opportunity to fuel my creativity by organizing several "theme" events, fashion shows and fundraisers that generated thousands of dollars.

My hobby caused me to abandon my legal studies and aspirations in favor for a Certificate and Career in Public and Media Relations Marketing.

Now residing in Toronto, after graduation, I quickly climbed the trenches holding different "Marketing/PR" positions in the Fashion, Food, Professional Development and Interactive Amusement industries.

Each role gave me the chance to observe the very best, step-up and perfect my marketing/sales, negotiation, communication, interpersonal and leadership skills.

"Walking my talk" and leading by example, in November, 1996, I founded PRIME TIME PR– a boutique marketing/PR firm fashioned after leading PR firms that provided similar services – only it was primarily geared towards independents, smaller companies and book authors who were often neglected by larger firms and their publishers.

With my colleagues' and client's respect and a few prestigious awards behind me, I boldly brought PR's many faces and facets to restaurateurs, retailers, lawyers, financial planners, chiropractors, psychotherapists, dentists, professional organizers, outdoor enthusiasts, art dealers, artists, dating services, resorts, pharmaceutical representatives, professional speakers, cell phone distributors, as well as a few politicians and celebrities.

Deemed "The PR Princess," I revolutionized industry standards, educated the business masses about PR's tremendous benefits and made PR Marketing more accessible to those who didn't have an advertising budget in excess of $50,000 and needed it the most.

I was also the first to introduce a PR club with pay-per-placement alternatives in the Canadian market place and upon completing my Competent Toast Master (CTM) designation, devised a series of Marketing/PR talks that I delivered at various venues across the GTA.

The launch of PRtalk (Canada's only online PR magazine), media appearances and my regular marketing/PR columns published in various newspapers and magazines soon followed.

I spent my days...

- Arranging client's publicity strategy, media contact list, media placements, speaking gigs & book tours.
- Determining their story line, unique selling point & call to action.
- Developing their press materials, blog, e-Zine & newsletter content.
- Scripting, story boarding & preparing them to take control of their media interviews, film videos and commercials
- Properly leveraging their exposure.

By night, I was on set as an extra-s in block-buster movies as well as landed two TV roles in Canadian productions. Filming lasted into the wee hours and began to conflict with business. Once again, I had to make a choice.

I remained running my own PR firm for years.

You might think I "had it all" and was living the glamourous life. Red carpets, limo rides, A-list parties, fine restaurants, buying whatever I desired and globe-trotting definitely had its perks!

However, my life as a publicist wasn't entirely a bed of roses. Conditioned in the "Male" success model, I catered to my clients every whim, worked day and night pulling them out of crisis and took many risks. Shedding more than a few tears, many times I wanted to give up and go work for an agency or TV station. But my passion, commitment, determination, and integrity pushed me on.

Until years of going it alone, not setting boundaries, sleeping three hours a night, "yo-yo" dieting and feeling like I was really cut-out to do something else caught up with me – left me with one failed relationship after another, never having the family I always wanted, weight issues, as well as a serious and chronic illness.

Burnt out and sick at the pinnacle of my career, I was forced to slow down and take on fewer clients. My income dwindled as I struggled to stay afloat and pay for my treatments and medications with no health coverage. Nearly $40,000 in debt, I felt ashamed, isolated, lost, hurt, and angry with myself and all the lifestyle changes I suddenly had to make. This severely affected my self-esteem, self-worth, and sense of identity.

The only way back UP was to…

- Delve deep with my soul and determine what mattered to me most.

- Love, accept, trust, and believe in myself no matter what.

- Live life on my terms with no apologies or excuses.

- Let my talents flow naturally while I transitioned into what I now consider my true calling – Janette Burke, "Your Media Marketing Mentor" - Producer, Janette Burke Productions, Host/Creator Janette's I'm Every Woman! TV, Video/Media Marketing Mentor, Speaker and Author.

I consider this experience a gift, since it allowed me to mature, receive tremendous support from friends, family, mentors, and spot and seize new opportunities including…

- Having many more of my articles published as well as my own PR column appear in a GTA newspaper over four years.

- Writing *67 Plus Ways to Promote Your Business & Make Money <u>Today!</u> - Proven Tricks of the Trade for Catching Customers and Becoming a Marketing Magnet.*

- Moving from behind the camera to where I always felt I truly belonged...to in front of it initially with "The Magnetic Marketing Moment" - my fifteen minute monthly marketing segment that first aired on Toronto's #1 Internet Radio TV Station.

- Joining "Liquid Lunch," a lifestyle & business show, where in addition to doubling my segment, I served as co-host the 3rd Monday of every month from April 2010 until February 2012. Highlights included planning shows & topics, booking guests, doing show notices & promo, being exposed to the "behind the scenes" technology, posing interesting questions, ad-libbing, doing my own hair & make-up, selecting wardrobe, meeting & interviewing local business owners, professionals, authors, musicians, performers, comedians, TV Show Hosts, politicians, members of the Media, fundraisers, coaches, consultants & celebs, as well as twice working the Red Carpet at TIFF (Toronto International Film Festival).

- Embracing my femininity and conducting business in the Feminine Success Model.

- Creating and Hosting three seasons of "I'm Every Woman! TV", taking an investigative approach to Women's Issues from both men and women guest perspectives and providing a forum for open discussion.

- Partnering on "The Video Marketing Machine" — a video marketing company that provides A-Z "Camera Ready" training, studio production and promotional push for clients who want to shoot professional videos for their websites, blogs, e-Zines and events or start their own online TV shows — and let the world know how amazing they are.

- Becoming an all-around advocate for Women's rights and issues. I'm on a mission to empower women to be all they can and pursue their dreams while embracing balance and preserving their femininity. I simply want to enrich and enhance Women's lives personally and professionally and give them the motivation, courage, and tools they need to muster anything!

- Taking over production of Janette's I'm Every Woman! TV this past August for Season 4, filming and airing forty-six episodes covering an array of Women's issues.

- Having the privilege of conducting over 300 interviews including those I did with well-known celebrities.

While I still frequent karaoke two or three times a week, dance and sing in shows hosted by my dear friend, an international entertainer and magician, knowing how to unleash that "certain something" that distinguishes them and mesmerizes their audience, today my primary purpose is to successfully get my clients past their fears of being on-camera, "tooting their own horn" and extending their brand.

I do this by combining Video (the new TV) with Social Media (the new PR), my expertise in Traditional Media and PR training and interviewing skills to help CEO'S, Small Business Owners, Professionals, Coaches, Consultants, Speakers, Book Authors, Artists, Chefs and even a few Celebrities find the confidence to clearly convey their message with the world, break-through the barriers to video and media success, look and sound their very best and gain the visibility they need to effectively publicize and promote their products and services.

Impacting my female viewers' lives personally and professionally with the guests and topics that I feature on Janette's I'm Every Woman! TV, I also help Women Entrepreneurs understand the value of video media marketing, as well as the trends that help them get known and take them from being their industry's best-kept secret to a recognized expert.

Quoting one of my favorite songs and groups, I "Don't stop believing" and neither should you!

Before Janette Burke became an Internet Reality Talk TV Producer, TV Show Host, Video/Media Marketing Consultant and Trainer, advocate of Women's Rights and Issues, and champion to Women in Business, she spent 17 years behind the camera as the Founding Publicist of Prime Time PR and Editor of PRtalk, Canada's only online PR magazine. Today, Janette shares her experience and helps you find the confidence you need to clearly convey your message and break through your biggest barriers to VIDEO & MEDIA success. She understands how to unleash that "certain something" that will mesmerize your audience.

www.janetteburke.com

CHAPTER 4   Margareth Nyakambangwe

Test Of Faith

Hebrews 11:1-3 defines faith as: *"Now faith is the assurance of things hoped for, the conviction of things not seen. For by it the people of old received their commendation. By faith we understand that the universe was created by the Word of God, so that what is seen was not made out of things that are visible"* (NKJV).

My life's journey is full of surprises and mysteries. Born in a Christian family of four; two girls and two boys, unfortunately, one of my brothers is now late. We were practising Christians though my father wasn't. He enjoyed his beer and cigarettes. We attended different churches at a time depending on which city we moved to. My mother, being a social worker, the nature of her job caused us to move around the country. My education at a mission school ignited my faith in God. As an adult, I changed my settings about my faith, from being a mere Christian to a born-again. I was aware of what I wanted in life, and this came with a lot of challenges.

With faith, you have to take bold steps, agree with yourself that you are going to pursue your belief in faith, come what may. Do not be intimidated when you face challenges during your journey. In my journey of faith with God, I faced many trials. I don't know how I managed to go through them all at the time but now I know it was the willpower that I had instilled in myself. Matthew 19:26 says *"... with man this is impossible, but with God all things are possible."*

My faith was tested in a great way beyond my scope. I lost everything. I lost my mother in June 2007; that was the biggest blow in my life. It was too soon for me to lose her. My mother's death was the hardest moment of my life. It took me time to accept her death. I kept hoping it was a dream and that one day I would wake up from the nightmare. That's the time I reflected on my life and I left everything in the hands of God.

A few years later, that was followed with a series of events which were beyond my scope. Whatever challenge you can think of or name, I went through it. First, I lost my job; that was the beginning of misery. I had gone through bereavement after losing my mother and brother in a space of three months. Those were followed by joblessness, financial loss, homelessness, broken relationships, and many other failures. There was no immune booster to these experiences in my life, but it was just definite that I had to go through this refinery until I became a better mould. I was homeless for two years. I slept in the streets of London with my car as my mobile home. People used to say if you want anything, go to Margareth's car. They had no idea why I had everything available in my car. I was rejected by everybody because I was jobless and homeless.

I give credit to four loyal people who stood by me during the test of my life. For at least two years my children missed school for a month or two every term due to my failure to pay the school fees in time but I thank God He gave my children wisdom. They performed very well despite their absence from school. I experienced extreme humiliation at every turn of my faith; by people who should have stood by me. Nonetheless, this didn't bother me. It was the time I also learnt who was who in my life.

The secret that I learnt about faith and belief is to be positive even in a very awkward, negative, or difficult situation. Once you believe, you will overcome any failure or hardships. I always believed things would be alright one day. You might find yourself in a situation whereby you are crying, trying to understand why all these misfortunes are happening to you and you might also be asking God why He would allow this to happen to you. I had an answer to this that my mother had taught me over the years. When my grandfather died, I was so depressed. Being very close to my grandfather, you can imagine. At the time, my mother asked me, "To whom should it have happened if not you? Whose grandfather could have died in his place?" This was food for thought. Right now in every situation I always ask myself that question: "If it's not me, who should go through this?" It made me a stronger person and got me to understand that in life, we go through phases or seasons but they will come to pass.

In the midst of all this, I lost my mother which marked an end to an era; losing a great woman who influenced my life. At one point I asked myself, "What have I done wrong?" I had no answer to that question. You take stock of your life and you don't find any shortfall. It's just you going through the refinery and at the end of it you become a tougher person. You will be able to understand and deal with any situation. This helps you to comfort someone going through the same situation. I have learnt not to worry but to be positive in every situation; good or bad.

I had huge debts but how I acquired them, I had no idea. I was very worried thinking how I was going to clear them. Finally one day, I stopped worrying and I just assured myself that God was going to settle them. From that moment in my life I was free. I didn't bother myself about the brown envelopes. I would just open them and just say, "God is in control." Most of them were completely written off, some I just had to pay a quarter of what was owed. That was amazing!

To the reader, I hope my story will enlighten or inspire you. No matter how dark the night is, dawn will always come. No matter how long the night is, it will soon be morning. In life, whatever you are going through, be they trials and tribulations, they will soon come to an end. Have great faith, believe, and you will receive your blessings. Do not allow fear to conquer your thoughts. Have a positive mind even when you are walking in the shadows of death. Above all, be filled with thankfulness. Invest in yourself because knowledge is power. When you act on it, nobody can take that from you. Get yourself a coach, mentor, or join a Mastermind alliance group that can help you go through your goals. You need a mentor or a good friend who makes you accountable to your own life. Someone who acts as a mirror; who can even give you constructive criticism in good faith in order for you to change your habits, attitude, etc. Above all, forgive, forget, and move forward. Find inner peace within yourself. Let bygones be bygones. Your faith in God is the most important pillar in your life.

Never give up on your dreams even if you put them on hold for a while. Rekindle your goals and move on. Do not allow people to steal or make you revive their own dreams or goals. Your faith is your pillar. The greater your faith is, the stronger you become and nothing can bring you down. Always ask God for wisdom, for wisdom carries everything on board. Whatever trial you must go through, always have faith in God.

Margareth Nyakambangwe is a Registered General Nurse, specializing in the Ophthalmic field, and has vast experience in Emergency Nursing. She is a mentor, entrepreneur, and an independent beauty consultant. She is the CEO and Owner of Alice Mambinge Ltd and the Founder of Alice Mambinge Foundation. She completed a coaching course in March 2015. Margareth is a philanthropist and is committed to helping young and talented underprivileged children to achieve their ambitions in education and sports. She is a mother of two boys and whilst not working or supporting her projects, she enjoys voluntary work, reading, traveling, cooking and baking.

akmambinge@gmail.com
twitter@magnum2tj

VISION TIP   Elizabeth Ann Pennington

How To Have A Balanced Vision

My vision as a Best-Selling International author and Certified Life Coach is to reach as many people as possible, helping them to heal – mind, soul, and body. My wish is to help them understand why they have low self-esteem or why they feel lost, confused, or unloved.

No one is perfect. You may feel powerless and unworthy. With all the outside influence we experience, it's easy to drift away from our plans and lose focus on our dreams. It's common for us to try to be what we think others want us to be. We view ourselves through the eyes of others .We sometimes wish we could be like them. When we divide mind from soul and body, we lose control of our decisions. We stop living our dream and start living theirs. You are a valuable individual just as you are – beautiful and unique.

 It's never too late. Sometimes we feel it's too late to accomplish the dream we had planned for our future. Things happen in life to knock us off our path. We must get a clear picture of the why and how we have gotten off the path before we can get back on. If you need help finding your way, don't feel weak by letting pride get in your way. Ask for assistance.

Conquer any fear you may have. Take one step at a time to build your confidence and courage. With focus and determination on your part, you'll begin to see the possibilities for your future.

Forgiveness will get you there. Rejuvenate your entire soul by making peace with yourself and those you feel have stood in your way. Holding onto a grudge will keep you stuck where you are. Without forgiveness, you cannot heal your mind, soul, and body. Forgive yourself first; then you will be able to forgive others.

Don't get in a hurry. This is your life. Take time to read each story written by the authors inside this book, *Living Without Limitations – Vision Quest*, compiled by Anita Sechesky. Build on each author's experience to learn how to think outside the box. While adapting to your new journey, find comfort in knowing you are not alone. How will it look to you when you have your mind, soul, and body in sync?

What are you waiting on? Take the first step towards your healing today.

CHAPTER 5   Monica Kunzekweguta

Write It Down

August 2013, I was preparing for a seminar to motivate a team of network marketers' men and women. As I scanned through my old note books looking for relevant material to use, I felt a quick rush of goose bumps all over my body, and the hair at the back of my head stood on its ends. The shock sent a cold shiver down my spine. This was not brought on by fear, but by realizing the power of writing one's vision down as clear and as detailed as possible. At the time of writing in March 2007, I felt kind of silly, and could hear my inner voice saying, "Joker, how are you going to be that, or achieve that? You don't even believe it yourself!" I wrote it down anyway. I managed to ignore the voice because I was fired up and energized by the leadership program I was taking. The Coaches and Facilitators talked about nothing except, "What is Possible!"

While glancing at, and inspecting my notes, this is what I read in notation form:

My Future: (March2007)

- Full of love where I am fighting for everyone to win.
- Have happy people around me whose lives are fulfilled because they also know what is possible for them.
- Be committed to my work, relationships, and humanity.
- This is the human being I am going to be...Loving, Generous, Passionate, Listening and Honouring.
- The ability to distinguish reality from what isn't real.

These words represented what I wanted to be and to experience: integrity, dignity, passion, compassion, grace, and transformation. Resultantly, I became emboldened to embark on a personal vision quest, and the subsequent narration of them here is just but a synopsis of that endeavour.

What had shocked me was the clarity and detail of the vision I had. I was living it! I knew that was what I wanted to do, but I had no idea there was a profession called Life Coaching. As I set out looking for someone to be my mentor, I serendipitously came across an online school which met all my needs. Over a period of time, I took courses and trained be to a Life Coach. After completing my studies, and with hindsight, I realized how this enabled me to do everything listed in the notes above. Yet still, during the course of my studies, what had made the experience so powerful and instilling a lot of confidence in me was the positive feedback I received from my fellow coaching students and my instructor. I knew that this was my life's purpose and destiny, because to me coaching was not just a career, it was a way of being. In retrospect, I have always felt like a giver and when I did that, I did not hold back. My passion has always been about seeing other people reach their unlimited potential. As an attribute, I thrive on witnessing other people grow and transform into whomever or whatever they want to be. As it so happens, I am currently compiling a book where the key areas of focus for the authors is their unlimited potential, self-value, and individuality. This gave me ample opportunities to mentor and encourage all my co-authors to do their best. I have learnt so much going through the challenges of building my team. This has been a huge benefit to me as my vision unfolds stage by stage.

While always a giver, I admit to the readers that I have not always been the person to spur others to their fullest potential, and nothing was as clear and so powerful. In fact the opposite could be true. My focus was mainly on WHY things weren't thriving; relationships, friendships, business, projects, and work. I wasn't happy; I was weighed down by regret about situations where I thought I could have taken action sooner or taken an initiative to live my life fully. I blamed myself for not being adventurous enough, being closed in, and feeling powerless. I failed to realize that everything I needed came from within and not from anyone else. I lacked confidence and remained in the same job which I no longer enjoyed. I was intimidated by stepping out of my comfort zone.

My problems were numerous; it was as if I was a magnet for trouble. It's true what they say - you attract more of what you focus on. FEAR was my demise. I worried that my tenants might not pay me rent, and that's exactly what I got! I ended up supporting grown-up strangers for a number of months and refused to leave. While all this drama was playing itself out, the mortgage lenders naturally expected my payment in full every month. I had to pay out of my pocket, which left me just managing to survive. If anyone knows living in the red, you need not look further. I spent all my money before I even earned it. But ironically, this made me realize and know that something needed to change drastically, and for the better. This was followed by fighting to secure two of my properties which I almost lost in the same year. All this stress took its toll on my health; I developed respiratory problems and sinuses which affected my ability to taste, my sense of smell, and hearing, for a while.

This was now a direct threat to my coaching and speaking career. I was convinced I had developed lung cancer, and being referred to the Lung Cancer Clinic gave me mixed emotions. I was so desperate to have a name for this strange illness which was now affecting my whole being. I resolved to accept that after many years of working in a residential setting before they designated smoking areas had finally caught up with me. I made several visits to the ENT (Ear, Nose and

Throat) clinic, but the specialist too could not come up with a sound diagnosis. It must be all the years of carrying the abnormal load of anger, lack of trust, regret, hate, feeling disempowered whilst putting up a front, and wearing a mask for the longest time that I can attribute it to. When you carry all that, you never feel beautiful. You see, when we get wrapped up in our own circumstances and concerns, we lose sight of what's possible. We settle for less and essentially adapt to things as they are. We fail to value ourselves. Lack of confidence and holding back go hand in hand. I did not believe in myself and didn't think I had it in me, let alone sharing anything of value.

It becomes clear that when the wholeness and completeness of who we are is jeopardized, however small, it begins to alter us, even if at first it's imperceptible. We might experience a sense of discomfort; spend time defending, explaining, or pointing fingers; find ourselves tolerating a level of unworkability that we might not normally put up with. Because this happens in small increments, we do not fully get the kind of impact it has on things not working in our lives as we carry on compromising. Once we reach that stage, we lose our power because are just focusing on surviving rather than living our lives to the fullest potential. We delay our growth and development in many areas and lose a huge chunk of our time here on earth, living without a purpose.

To digress for a moment, and for emphasis, I will add that I have noticed something different about how we are, and how society is. We have developed a culture and desire for instant gratification. Whether it is in relationships, business, and projects or even prayer, we seek to attain our results in minutes. No one is interested in investing time to understand that "special" person; to have a relationship where both parties are fulfilled. In business, few are prepared to face or deal with the challenges of building a business. Nobody cares to understand why things are this way or simply recognize the law of cause and effect.

Look at the life of a butterfly for example. Their complete life cycle follows four stages, each one looks different and serves a unique purpose in the life of this amazing insect. It starts from egg to larval stage, pupal stage, then finally a butterfly, which is the adult stage. Depending on the type of butterfly, the life cycle maybe anywhere from one month to a whole year. At no stage should the development be compromised or there won't be a butterfly. When you see it at the larval (or caterpillar) stage, you would never imagine it emerging as the most beautiful insect you have ever seen. Also when you think of the pupa, it looks as if the caterpillar may just be resting, but inside of it a lot of action is taking place. The caterpillar is rapidly changing. The same is true with us: we need to do a lot of work inside to become the amazing persons we want to be.

When a human being is conceived, it takes nine months for the baby to develop to full term. If born too early, complications may arise, or worse. Development and growth are inevitable processes of life. Before we reach or can attain certain levels of success, there are stages we need to go through. If that is not followed by growth, it presents some serious repercussions. Take people who win a lottery. We have seen countless TV programs where the winners have lost all the money in short span of time. In some countries, winners of huge sums of money are offered financial counseling and training. Who would have ever thought that winning a lotto windfall required some form of educating, but it does. There are patterns and habits we need to give up on in order to succeed. I am encouraging you to keep your dream and vision alive. Do whatever it takes to achieve your goals. Never stop trying or doing your best.

Your vision or life's purpose maybe unclear, but pay attention to those things that cause you to lose track of time. You can also invest in some coaching so that you are supported to work out your life's purposes before you lose more time.

I often wonder, what happened to deferred gratification? Why have we lost the ability to put off the satisfaction of present desires to gain greater satisfaction in the future? I have read biographies of successful people and most of them indicate that they began to achieve success in their businesses after several years. Despite challenges and setbacks, one has to stay focused and persevere.

A momentary pause here might be useful, if not for anything, but just to remind the reader that what might have seemed like a digression earlier, can now be married. So my transformation began when I decided to further my studies. As it happens, my first assignment was to write an essay on a particular book that explores quantum physics, the supernatural, and our part in shaping our own destiny. As I did my research in preparation for the essay, I realized that I had two of the most essential books in my own library which I had bought seven years earlier…yes SEVEN, and had not bothered to read – they were still new. I came to understand that for many years all I had was intention but never took any action. Two other Best-Selling publications are what I call "life manuals," in there are written the basic life principles. If you live by those ideologies, your life will be less stressful and you will master ways of achieving your goals and staying focused. You will be able to become an extraordinary human being.

It became apparent that I was not the only one who fell in this category. Gradually, I understood that procrastination, if it goes on for years, becomes a debilitating habit which eats away at your life and suppresses your real potential. The cycle goes somewhat like this. Something happens and you get extremely frustrated and feel determined to change your situation. You set out on a path or mission to do just that. You look at every business opportunity, go on Amazon or any book store and buy the best Inspirational, motivational, and self-help books available. You read the first few chapters, get this sense of achievement, tell yourself that it is indeed easy, but never implement a single thing. The scenario is too familiar to millions. Ten years later you are still on the same spot or worse off. The question to ask is "What is missing?" In my case it was encouragement, focus, and accountability. I wanted to go it alone, I never wanted anyone to take credit for my success, and yet great leaders relied upon the power of collaboration and masterminding. Napoleon Hill wrote, *"Every mind needs friendly contact with other minds, for food of expansion and growth; the coordination of knowledge and effort of two or more people, who work toward a definite purpose, in the spirit of harmony."* He continues… *"No two minds ever come together without thereby creating a third, invisible intangible force, which may be likened to a third mind [the master mind]". Joining a mastermind group was an eye opener for me. I learnt the value of brainstorming where everyone in the group wants nothing but success for the others. When I was involved working on a big project, its magnitude scared me. I was ready to run but the support I got from my group was great. I learned a valuable lesson – I had reached the quitting zone, which happens just before one succeeds. I got to understand that it was a normal process. Can you imagine the number of people who give up at this stage?*

I realized my passion and purpose when I pursued my Life Coaching training. I went on to co-author in two books which became Best-Sellers within hours of being published. My career began to shape itself and I landed on an international platform as a speaker. When you free your mind and trust God, miracles begin to manifest. I discovered that when you truly forgive yourself and others, and get closure to those relationships which were significant in your life, you create space for other possibilities. You make room for genuine love for self and others, and you become open to receiving love. Forgiveness comes from bringing to a stop the comparisons between yourself and others, judging yourself and others, feeling sorry for yourself, and regretting past mistakes. Know that you made the best decision under the circumstances, and based on the information you had at the time.

Start to notice the power of forgiveness, acceptance, and allowing yourself to be coached. It is important to get closure and make it complete with any relationship. If that does not happen, you will be left wondering about stolen years; it's difficult to move on. I quit focusing on who owed me what and how much. I realized I was consumed by that and focused on lack rather than abundance. It was hard to let go as it was part of my story for many years. Quitting was the only way I needed to create room for new possibilities. It was when I decided to let go that I started to see major changes. Doors which were locked, and those which I didn't even know existed and could be accessible to me, started to open. I am now being invited to speak at International conferences and am even headhunted to fill positions in political parties. But I know my passion and also know where I will serve my destiny and purpose better. I now own my power; it is a process. I won't say I have reached my potential just yet but I am willing and open to learn. Like any muscle, it needs exercising to maintain its function and to excel. It takes courage to live in a transformed way, to wrestle with our own resistance, to give up on mediocrity, to live consistent with what we know is possible in being human. It all results from making a choice. Creating a breakthrough, stepping out, and taking new grounds requires disturbing our old conversations of self-criticism and self-doubt.

I know I can create. I am currently compiling my first book *"A Woman's Beauty Is the Depth of Her Soul!"* This is giving me numerous chances to sharpen up on my leadership skills. *A Woman's Beauty* encompasses my vision. Act To Grow, my coaching business, is a constant reminder of how taking action is paramount to one's success. In five years' time, *A Woman's Beauty* will be providing Life Coaching, Mentoring, and Speakers' platforms. I am working on a clothing line which will be launched this summer. This is yet another miracle which manifested when I least expected. This is the very reason why reading though my detailed vision gave me the chills. It was the moment I realized the power of stating your intentions and writing them down.

A vision I had in 2007 is now a reality. I am living it in 2015, but it's not the end because my vision remains alive and evolves as I am getting more and more extraordinary results. I will stay on this path and follow my "Vision Quest" because once I had mastered it, it became a way of life. Now I need to enroll others and encourage them to seek their destiny and life's purpose!

Monica Kunzekweguta, a sociology graduate, is an International Best-Selling Author, Certified Life Coach, International Speaker and Mastermind facilitator. Owner and CEO at Act To Grow Life Coaching, she is also the Director of A Woman's Beauty, an organization which focuses on Personal Coaching, workshops, and Speakers' platforms. Monica is the Project Founder of Inspiration for Kids International charity, providing library books to children living in rural Zimbabwe. She co-authored *"Living Without Limitations – 30 Stories to Heal Your World"*, *"#LOVE – A New Generation of Hope Continues..."*, and is currently compiling her first book *"A Woman's Beauty Is the Depth of Her Soul"*.

www.awomansbeauty.co.uk
https://www.facebook.com/monica.kunzekweguta

CHAPTER 6   W.A. Read Knox

You Can Manifest Your Desires

This is a manifestation story about a weeklong effort to catch an Atlantic salmon in the Glen Etive River in the Highlands of Scotland. The river is not very big and runs westward from the Scottish highlands about twelve miles to the Atlantic Ocean. It flows through what may be one of Scotland's most beautiful Glens, with treeless green grass covered mountains surrounding it on all sides, except its pathway to the sea. The river is the home for a run of Native Atlantic Salmon that average ten to fifteen pounds in size. These fish can only make it up the river to spawn as far as the very deep "Home Pool" that's located before a waterfall too tall for the fish to continue. This pool was also several hundred yards from the Home (Small Castle) and the Fleming Estate that my father-in-law had rented for several weeks specifically to fish this river every day with the family. He had invited us all to visit as it was their 50th wedding anniversary and the whole family came to enjoy the week.

The first morning we all assembled in the dining room and had a big Scottish Breakfast of toast, coffee, and bacon. Then we went to the home pool to practice casting with our designated fly rods. Now I had been Salmon fishing with a fly rod many times before, but here on this river some very special extra-long bamboo rods were used to get the fly out into the water a greater distance from the shore. Here, one fished from the river bank, not from a boat. The bamboo rods weighed substantially more and it took both hands and arms to coordinate smooth casts. Once I got adjusted, it was like using any other rod, only much more cumbersome. As the hours went on, the heavier these rods became, or so it seemed. I was repeatedly casting with no fish in sight, but the desire to catch something was building one cast at a time.

I don't think that there are words to describe the disappointment I felt after wandering slowly down the river all morning, casting fly after fly into what looked like the perfect water, but never catching, or even seeing, a fish. Everyone had been assigned a Ghillie or guide who knew the river and would take us to their favorite spots to catch fish. My Ghillie was named Allister and he was very sure that he was taking me to the best spots every day. I, like everyone in our party, hadn't seen a fish all day and was beginning to make suggestions like, "Let's go fish down there." or "I bet the other side of the river is better fishing." My father-in-law however was not dismayed and told us about the fish he had caught before we arrived and that the water level was the perfect height for the fish to get up into the river. He said that here you had to work for every fish, that your shadow could spook them, and every little detail had to be just right in order to be successful. The Ghillies all told us stories about the Scottish lore's of this land and river as we had our picnic lunches.

That night in the middle of a dark driving rainstorm, my father-in-law entered the house with a ten pound salmon he had just caught in the home pool. I will never forget the look of triumph and the smile on his face. The rest of us were drinking cocktails exclaiming what a waste of time it was...fishing in a downpour...in the middle of the night. Imagine the surprise to see him pop thru the doorway, Salmon in hand, and proclaim himself the best fisherman of the group.

Everyday ended the same way – my father-in-law catching the only fish and the rest of us trying harder and harder to catch one too. On our last day I, being the rebel that I am, decided to fish the only place I hadn't yet – at the mouth of the river where it meets the ocean. My Ghillie, named Allister, tried to persuade me from going there because, "There aren't any fish there", but then decided if that's where I wanted to go, I could go without him.

After about an hour's walk, I arrived at the river's end all alone with the beauty of the Glen Etive and the ocean. I recall saying, "God, if you are here, then send me a sign." Immediately, a salmon jumped totally out of the water right in front of me! Now it didn't take me long to get my rod ready as I became enthused and excited that there was at least one fish to be casting to. I chose a new fly to tie on my line and flung it in the direction the fish had jumped. Suddenly, the rod was almost being dragged out of my hands. I had a fish on! Because I hadn't brought my net with me, I had to fight this fish until he was so tired, I could land him in the rocks at the river's edge. I was so thrilled and exuberant that I had succeeded with my goal.

Altogether, I landed ten salmon that day where "No fish" were supposed to be. The moral of this short story is to believe that anyone can follow their instincts and manifest their desires.

W. A. Read Knox was born in Buffalo, New York and graduated from Yale University with a Bachelor of Arts degree. He is a Residential Realtor in Phoenix, Maryland, is married, has five children, and works with his oldest daughter. Read is an International Best-Selling author, having written a chapter in each of the *Living Without Limitation* series of books compiled by Anita Sechesky. He is a life and health, business, and athletic coach. Read is an entrepreneur with experience in mortgage banking, real estate, residential construction lending and land development, banking, aviation (private pilot), trucking and transportation.

knoxread@yahoo.com
facebook.com/read.knox

VISION TIP   Angela T. Muskat

How To Forgive The Unforgiveable

"Forgiveness realizes that there is nothing to forgive!" Author unknown.

I love this quote, and every time I am feeling resentful I call it back as a reminder.

Holding my share of judgment, blame, resentment, and guilt picked up throughout my life, I had to do some inner work on forgiveness. I came to understand that unforgiveness feeds victim consciousness. If we want to live our lives up to our full potential, we are better off to let go of the judgment, the grudges, the blame, the resentment, and the guilt. Even though some of us have traveled through literal hell, revisiting those old wounds every single day just robs us of our life force energy and leaves us drained, tired, and exhausted.

Looking at the truth of what is will help us progress. We cannot undo what has been done. We can never make it go away. What we can do is accept that it did happen, forgive, and be at peace with it.

That's easier said than done you think...and you are right. But the willingness to forgive will start the process and we'll be guided from there. Forgiveness doesn't only happen inside our heads. It is a process that happens on a cellular level.

The journey of forgiveness starts with forgiving and loving ourselves. The more we are able to progress there, the easier it will be to forgive others.

On an energetic level, we become what we make wrong. The "wrong making" of all the past abandonment, rejections, abuse, et cetera just keeps us trapped in the same repetitive pattern.

Once we take responsibility for what happened, as terrible as it has been, forgiveness happens. Taking responsibility does not rationalize or justify any happenings, it just takes us out of the circle of victimhood into the empowered, compassionate, and loving part of ourselves.

To get there, a willingness to feel our suppressed feelings and emotions that came with the event, and that we perceive as unforgivable, is crucial. This process will free up stuck energy and move us beyond, into a higher awareness with a new perception. Once we perceive events differently, we start to be able to recognize how everything that happens in our lives is actually serving us, and no matter how hard it seems at the time, life is always on our side.

CHAPTER 7   Nikki Clarke

If You Can See It, You Can Achieve It!

People ask me time and time again, "So, what's your story? How did you get into starting your own talk show?" The simple answer remains, it took vision and hard work. If you can see it, you can achieve it. Giving up is not an option.

Growing up in an all French neighborhood in the east end of Montreal, as the only Jamaican family, or better yet, the only black family, I was the brunt of racial attacks on a regular basis. The assaults went from verbal barrages of the N word and spitting to punches. My first taste of racism was at the tender age of four-years-old. My parents became very protective of me, sheltering me from anymore hurt. As a result, I was not allowed to go to friends' homes. They had to come to mine where they could be monitored under my parents' watchful eye. When the children weren't allowed to come to my home, I found ways to entertain myself instead of being alone. I had a rich fantasy life and loved the TV sitcoms of the 70's. I would sit in front of the TV concentrating on the conversations. I would then practice my new words and accents on my dolls, who became my captive audience. I wanted this kind of attention. I wanted to be loved and admired, the object of everyone's affection. I worked hard at this ability to imitate others going over scripts in my mind in front of my doll. This talent would serve me well later as I developed it into acting in the years to come.

When I was twelve-years-old, my parents bought me a typewriter for my birthday. Most girls my age were given dolls for their birthdays, but my parents saw that I had talent and wanted to develop my writing skills. I wrote my first song when I was seven and from then wrote poems to award-winning short stories. I also had that gift of gab. I loved to present in front of my class mates and often got the part of the lead in school plays. So if you marry the two, writing and public speaking, it would make perfect sense to have a career in television, so I thought. I saw an episode of this charismatic woman on television one day and was immediately drawn to her. I was twenty-one when I saw the *Oprah Winfrey Show* for the first time and I knew then what I wanted: to have my own talk show. She was like me. I could identify with her. She was a black woman trying to make sense of the world. She gave people a platform to share with others their authentic selves. I wanted to be a part of that and I became a fan ever since. So now that I was convinced I had what it took to be a talk show host, I had to convince others, namely my parents, and do the work.

I enjoyed my time as a student. Academically I was brilliant. I was always one step ahead of the class. However, I also resonated with the arts. I could sing, dance, write, and act – the challenge of being multitalented. Even when my parents wouldn't attend most of my performances in school, I pressed on for the sheer pleasure of performing. I loved being on stage and no amount of shaming or scarcity of cheerleaders would keep from it. I made that decision when I was twenty, a resolve that would insulate me from losing focus my entire life.

My parents wanted me to follow a career as a teacher, an accountant, or some other "secure" career. I understood what was expected of me. My parents believed that as a woman of color, the only way to overcome obstacles in the work place was to become the most educated and most qualified. They also wanted to spare me of a life of a hardship as a starving artist. "There is no security in performing," I would hear. I followed the expectation of pursuing a noble calling and became a teacher. I was an instructor in the Early Childhood Education program for ten years in College and I enjoyed it. Then in 2008, I ran out of the fuel that inspired me every day to prepare lesson plans, mold minds, and better yet, mark a copious amount of term papers. I needed a creative outlet. I came across an internet TV station in Toronto that was looking for new programs. I pitched an idea to the station owner about a show I called *AND THE BEAT GOES ON* that showcased Toronto talent. The station owner gave me the green light and there it began. I would dress in suits Monday to Friday for school and Saturday my alter ego, "Nixondamix" in jeans and cap would emerge. I interviewed artists and played musical videos. I filled my "soul cup "and went back to school recharged anticipating another amazing Saturday night at the station.

In 2009, I made a difficult decision to leave teaching. I loved it but I knew that I had to pursue this new found passion project. So without a safety net, I took a leap of faith. I handed in my resignation and cried like a baby for days. I was terrified and elated. I couldn't sacrifice one for the other. I had to give up something to focus on the other. That fortified my decision to leave teaching.

The show's audience grew internationally in a span of three years. It went from a Saturday night hobby to a business. I was interviewing local heroes and world class celebrities. Some days were amazing and some days were bleak. I wasn't prepared for the downside of starting a business. I'm not sure if anyone who ventures into full time entrepreneurship does. I knew that I had to follow my dreams and that if I had unyielding faith it would work out in the end. When my friends were working a nine to five shift, I was working a "wake up until I go to bed" grind. When others were attending parties, I was working. When my friends went on dates, I was alone in my office, working. While my friends had time to devote to their family, I had to divide my time finding ways to make money in order to make ends meet providing for my three children. I sacrificed friendships, my time, my health, and my family in the pursuit of making this show a success. I had to stick to my vision when certain members of my production team quit abruptly or turned on me when I wasn't able to provide any work for them. I had to pursue my vision when celebrity clients claimed they couldn't afford to pay the fees to the publicity company I started in 2009. There was a time when I had to face the decision to either eat or pay my bills. It wasn't easy. No one could have prepared me for family members and so called friends walking out of my life. Apparently, my ex-husband and his partner were planting poisonous seeds in my children's minds against me, claiming that I was an Obeah woman invoking magic to keep my ex-husband from finding work. Funny, I thought lack of initiative and poor attitude were his reasons.

In 2013, I met a man whom I dated for a few months. He was good-looking and charming. He came to all my show tapings. I thought, finally, my Stedman has come. I have someone in my life who understands, accepts, and truly supports me. The support turned into bursts of raging verbal abuse. One night as he was driving us to a Nikki Clarke Show interview, he yelled at me in the car that he would leave me if I didn't lose weight. I sat back stunned. I kept quiet holding back tears keeping my composure for the interview. When people emerged around us he would become loving and sweet, and then a bully behind closed doors. Two days after my birthday in December, when he called me in a screaming fit on the phone, I fought back. I told him I couldn't take his verbal abuse any longer and to stop contacting me. For a week, he repeatedly called and texted his apologies but it was too late. He went too far, and there was no going back. A few months later, I stumbled across his Facebook page and it threw me for such a loop. A few days prior to seeing his Facebook post, my cameraman suddenly quit working for me, claiming they had a special project that would be keeping them busy for a while. Well, it turns out that my ex-boyfriend started his own talk show and stole my cameramen. I closed my eyes. Can't give up. Giving up is not an option. The hurt won't last. This was a blessing in disguise.

My family and the friends slowly drifted away. The phone calls and visits became less frequent to none at all. I exchanged the comfortable life provided by a regular corporate paycheck to creating ways to making a living through my services in media, and spiraling downfall of other problems. My confidence was depleted. My self-esteem was low. I was isolated from others who judged me for my living situation and lack of stability. I turned to eating as a way to comfort myself and shopping to get that high I needed to medicate myself from the isolation and the pain I was experiencing. Why did I sign up for this again? Was this worth it? Many days I would cover my face with my hands as I sobbed heavily full of despair. I had gone too far to give up. I can't give up…

Between 2009 and 2011, my secret internal struggles of depression and anxiety from financial instability and the betrayal/loss of relationships, forced me to take a long, hard look at myself. I had to scrutinize myself from the outside in and truly examine my life. Why was I living what I felt was an incomplete life? Why was I making certain choices in my life? Why didn't I feel love? Why did I feel disconnected from others? Through it all, I would show up with others smiling and functioning well on the surface wearing a mask to hide my feelings of inadequacy and failure. When my cross felt too heavy to carry, I would get an email or phone call, congratulating me on what I was trying to do for the community and how I changed that person's life. I knew that was God sending an angel to help me. I realized that God was always around me waiting on me to ask for help. I believe that this hard journey helped me become closer to Him. In the unconditionally loving relationship I have with God,

I finally understand my purpose. I was born to facilitate platforms for others to share their messages of hope. My purpose has a great responsibility and challenges. However, it would all have meaning to someone at some time when they most needed it, just like when I needed it in my moments of despair and hopelessness.

After some time, I made a conscious shift. I spent a great deal of time becoming more self-aware by connecting with others in the field of human behavior and spiritual healers. I learned that I was creator of all my triumphs and tribulations. I was in control. I couldn't blame anyone else any longer because I created every situation I was in. I understood that my self-sabotaging, limiting beliefs were holding me back from what I wanted in life and that I had to make changes. The only way that I could heal from the past hurts was to have the courage to take off my mask first. This in turn would give people the guts to take off their masks and share from their true selves.

In October 2012, The Nikki Clarke Show was born from the need to practice what I was preaching of being authentic. The premise of the show was to invite people from all walks of life to share their heart stories, getting past the superficiality of how they accomplished what they did by overcoming the challenges in their lives. Living in Toronto, I have observed people looking for direction, affiliation, and love. There are many people in this city feeling disconnected. The goal of creating the show was to connect those people to kindred spirits or people with resources to get them the help they needed. "Build it and they will come" was the divine whisper I heard. The tagline of the show became "Transforming Lives, One Story at time." After some time, the reaction to the show was better than I thought. The model of creating a local program of awareness and authenticity took some people by surprise. The show was a refreshing change. People from all over Canada, the West Indies, Africa, Asia, and Europe were reaching out to me to find out how they could be a part of the show, either through sponsorship or to become guests. I felt the shackles of doubt fall off when the show was welcomed at an internationally recognized theme restaurant in downtown Toronto for its live taping in 2014.

The show was meeting a community need. People wanted their stories to be heard and others wanted to hear those stories to be uplifted and motivated. It's working, I thought. This is what the sacrifice was about. In May 2014, I founded the Nikki Clarke Network, a twenty-four hour online TV network of inspirational programming. I got to a point in my life when I was disgusted with all the negative images on TV. I wanted to create an alternative for viewers and a launching pad for emerging producers to get their talk shows into the stratosphere. I coached the content producers the ropes of online TV production by giving them direction in their show ideas and arranging the production framework. The network started with the flagship show, *The Nikki Clarke Show*, and now has up to 10 shows ranging from real estate, politics, music, spirituality, to wellness.

In 2015, I received the Woman of Honor Award, by the Black Business Professional Association, I was nominated for Best Media Personality by the Black Canadian

Awards, and was selected 100 Black Women in Canada to Watch. I humbly receive the awards and accolades remembering how, not too long ago, those early days of starting the business transformed me. Just like a butterfly, the metamorphosis from the cocoon to flight took time.

The show is now flourishing and I am leveraging others to have a voice through online TV. I am writing an anthology called *"Transforming Lives, One Story at a Time"*. I am expanding the Nikki Clarke Show in Jamaica, the USA, and Montreal. I started the Clarke Media Arts Program to mentor at risk youth video production. I am working with professional, loyal, crew members. I have strong bonds with genuine friends and the love for my family is constant although at times they were unsupportive. Forgiveness has freed me from the past. I chose to release toxic attachments, create healthier ones, and move on.

I have learned that there is no such thing as an overnight success. What appears as quick achievements were actually years of determination, sacrifice, blood, sweat, and tears that no one witnessed. I clung to my vision as a buoy in those days of flood when there was no land in sight. If you can see it, you can achieve it. Giving up is not an option.

Nikki Clarke was born in Jamaica and went from being a college professor to launching her talk show "The Nikki Clarke Show" in 2012. The show invites people from all walks of life to share their heart stories taped in front of a live audience. The award-winning Producer and International Motivational Speaker also launched her online TV network, www.nikkiclarkenetwork.com, in May 2014. Nikki produces a variety of online TV shows from real estate and world politics to women's wellness.

www.nikkiclarkenetwork.com
nikki@nikkiclarkeinc.com

PROTECTING

THE

VISION

CHAPTER 8   Anita Sechesky

Protecting The Vision

Have you ever felt like a situation knocked the wind out of you and you didn't know who, what, why, and where it came from? Maybe it was after you acknowledged something about your goals and dreams, and expected to have a cheering squad surround and lift you up on their shoulders. You had imagined them celebrating the very thought of such a powerful ambition and were secure in the knowledge that you had the love, wisdom, and support to back you all the way to fulfilling your dreams. However, that wasn't how it transpired and the consequences which remain from you stepping out of your comfort zone and sharing your precious vision has now left you feeling vulnerable and insecure. The very thought of planning and implementing any sort of action towards this beautiful vision has now left you feeling nauseous in the pit of your stomach. You don't know in which direction to move.

Well, thankfully you're not alone with this experience and you shouldn't beat yourself up about it. Too many individuals walk away disappointed, or even scarred so deeply, they never return to the drawing board or creative stage again, giving up altogether in bringing their vision to life. However, there are ways for you to protect your vision so that it never experiences any kind of disrespect and abuse. After all, your vision is an extension of who you are. It was conceived from your soul purpose and established in the universe once you took ownership of it. This is why many people are affected so deeply when they face negative criticism about their goals and dreams.

Understanding that the integrity of who you are deserves to be treated with respect will empower you to not accept harsh and cynical comments about your high standards and ambitions any longer. Once you have determined that your vision is not open for condemnation, you are stronger and aware when others may try to sabotage your vision. Many times, it's the people who are closest that hurt us the most, understandably because there are emotional soul ties in place. Although you may not want to damage your relationships with your loved ones by speaking your truth, they may not have the same level of respect towards you regardless. Remember this doesn't mean they don't love you, it just means they don't love the vison for you. Human beings are very complex and yet very transparent at the same time. What we see in others is often a reflection of what we're internalizing and instead of jumping to conclusions or becoming offended so easily, we should literally step back and examine our own hearts and intentions towards others. It's so easy to carry negativity and anger without realizing it's consuming us. But as we see how our perceptions are easily affected by the individuals we align ourselves with, we can better understand our thought processes.

So what I'm really trying to say is that we're all at risk to some degree of becoming "Vision Killers." If we don't recognize the environment we choose to be influenced by, we'll be no different than those who have done the same to us. I encourage you to be a "Vision Healer" and afford others the grace to be healed from the damage caused by negativity. Support people who have a goal and build them up. Listen and direct them to the resources they need to bring their vision to life. In doing so, you have secured the environment that's required for you to also grow and birth your vision.

CHAPTER 9   Kristine Gravelle-Rystenbil

Surprise! I'm A Leader And Visionary

January 2013 – It's 2 am…the house is quiet and my family's asleep. I like working after everyone's in bed because that's when my head is clearest.

Tonight my thoughts are troubled. I'm trying to come up with a creative idea for my business, but I'm stuck. I've been meditating a lot recently and think to myself, "Maybe If I still my thoughts, I can get a Divine answer to what I should focus on." I close my eyes and begin. As soon as my eyes are shut, I see an image in my mind that's immense! EVERYWHERE there's the expanse of Universe! I find myself catching my breath. In a split instant I get a *knowing* and I think, "Holy Smokes! I've just tapped into the Universal energy of feminine consciousness. I'm supposed to help shift feminine consciousness."

I know I'm getting direction from Higher Self (God), but I'm overwhelmed and start panicking. "Me? But, I'm just one person? Why me? This is too big for me." Stilling my thoughts again, I reply, "Okay. I'll do what you ask of me…one step at a time." After that mini-meditation, I decide to finish the work I need to do and go to bed. Life continues, but the vision stays fresh and constant in my mind.

January 2015 – "What you just shared with me is BIG!" says the voice on the other end of the phone. "You should consider putting this into a book."

I'm talking on the phone with an amazing woman I met at a conference in Toronto, two months earlier. Her comment comes just after I've shared with her what I've been working on over the past two years – *relationship and intuition coaching, and using Scientific Hand Analysis to tell women what their Life Purpose is.*

"Relationship, intuition, and purpose are three cornerstones in a woman's life," I reveal. "When a woman harnesses all three, she instantly steps into her fullest potential."

"I'm not sure if you know this, but I'm a publisher," the woman's voice at the other end of the line says. She describes her experience, then asks, "Kristine, will you own this vision and consider writing an anthology book where you invite twenty-nine other women to share their experience and wisdom on these three cornerstones?"

A lot flashes through my mind when she asks that question: Will my family laugh at me when I tell them I'm writing a book? Do I add one more project onto my insanely full plate? How do I get other women to join? I'm not a leader.

To bypass my mental chatter, I ask my Higher Self (my ultimate connection with God) and it immediately confirms, "*Yes! Do the book.*"(Note: I've been cultivating a relationship with my intuition since my early thirties, so when I ask my Intuition for direction on what I'm supposed to do, I implicitly trust and follow the answer I get, because it's ALWAYS right)

Over a nine-month period, I contact over four hundred women globally and share the vision of the book with them. Some join the project, some don't. Because the book is about the journey of women, I title it, *"Ruby Red Shoes – Empowering Stories of Relationship, Intuition and Purpose."*

As I search for women to participate in the project, any time I lose my momentum or feel frustrated, I think back to that January night in 2013, In an instant I feel the powerful Universal expanse, and I'm reminded that this project *must happen* and what my role is. I keep moving forward.

As the leader of the *Ruby Red Shoes* book, I feel humbled by the women who've joined the project – they're thankful to be part of this book, they're excited to share the vision with others, and they're happy that I'm leading the project.

Being in the role of leader is a new experience for me. I question my abilities, and ask myself whether I'm any good at it. I even question my vision and wonder if it's real. In moments like this, I remember the truth of it, "My vision was a gift from God. If I keep following His purpose for me, God will push me out of my comfort zone, to live life beyond what I imagine for myself. He'll even bring situations and people into my life to keep reinforcing I'm a leader until I believe it for myself."

And so it is.

With an extensive career and experience (25+ years in public and private sector) in Human Resources, Administration, Communications, Desktop publishing, Kristine Gravelle-Rystenbil is a Scientific Hand Analyst, Life Purpose and Potential Coach, Speaker, Author, Artist, Singer, and Advanced Energy Healer. As the Owner of KGR Hand Analysis and The Luv Chick, when Kristine's not coaching and supporting women, working on her latest project, or volunteering at her kids' school, she spends time with her husband and two children doing what she loves: watching movies, gardening, painting in her studio, reading, traveling and working on projects that inspire her.

www.kgr-handanalysis.com
https://www.facebook.com/HandAnalyst.KristineGravelleRystenbil?ref=hl

VISION TIP   Mélany Pilon

How To Live In The Moment

Are you caught up in life but not consciously living it? What's preventing you from living in the moment? The answer is your thoughts about the past and future, which interferes with your experience of living in the now. How do you escape thoughts of depression from the past and/or fears of the future? Simply by bringing your attention back to the present as soon as you are aware that your mind is drifting away.

Here are few tips to help you to remain in the moment.

Breathe. Your breathing has different patterns depending what mood you're in. Practice mindful breathing. This will relax you and bring you back into the moment.

Awareness. Once you become aware that your mind is drifting away in your thoughts, only then you can bring yourself back to the moment. To help yourself, use an affirmation like "I'm back."

Do one thing at a time. By multi-tasking, this enables you to completely engage yourself in the experience. Put your 100% focus and attention towards what you are creating.

Put some fun in your life. One of the reasons we drift away in our thoughts is because we're not enjoying ourselves in the moment. Memories and fantasies appeal more. Follow your excitement. Go out and act on your joy without hesitation, judgment, or by over-analyzing. Create fun and excitement for yourself. Smile, be kind, and do activities you enjoy.

Experience your senses. By paying attention to all your senses, you will be experiencing the moment. Feel the breeze, the rain, or the sun on your skin. Listen to the birds chirping. Smell the flowers. Look at the beauty of nature. Taste fresh cut fruits. And so on…

Set alarms, reminders, and make lists. By doing this, you won't have to constantly worry about being late for a meeting or missing something at the grocery store. This will help you to relax and enjoy your free time to its fullest.

Discover who you are and live by living in the here and now. Past and future are thoughts full of regrets and worries. We don't need to attach emotions to them as they don't exist and they keep us away from enjoying the greatness of the moment.

Practice Mindfulness. Every moment is a gift. Don't miss it by being away! Be in the now!

CHAPTER 10   Dr. Jacinth Tracey

How I Overcame Limiting Beliefs And Achieved Life Success

It's often been said that we live life forwards but understand it backwards. There is a definite truth to that adage with respect to my own experience. Looking back at a half-century of life is quite eye-opening. In retrospect, I can see how all the years of striving to develop myself intellectually, emotionally, spiritually, personally and professionally – and experiencing successes and failures along the way – have brought me to exactly where I was meant to be. From my current vantage point as a renowned women's leadership coach, corporate trainer, international speaker, and multiple best-selling author, all the paths that once seemed so divergent have converged into a cohesive and meaningful personal and professional life.

Who would have thought, certainly not a younger version of myself, that I'd be where I am at this stage in my life. The powerful, confident, self-determined person I am today is not the person I was in my younger years. Looking back I can see that for much of my early life, I was passive, full of fear and limiting beliefs, and frustrated about my inability to control various aspects of my life. But like all of us, I wasn't born that way. I became that person as a result of the childhood experiences that shaped my self-image and my perception about my ability to control my life outcomes.

We're all shaped by our social environment. From the day we're born, the first social influences that we encounter come from our immediate family unit. In fact, before we become teenagers and begin to think more independently, our family is the most important source of social influence on our emotional development and self-image. Sometimes the things that we learn about ourselves from our families are positive, and at other times they're negative. In my case, because I grew up in an authoritarian household (typical of middle-class Jamaican families in the 1960s) I was taught to be obedient, responsible, respectful, hard-working, and not to question authority. But that environment also taught me to suppress my own needs, to squash any feelings of anger or resentment, and to passively accept situations that were emotionally damaging. Research shows that children raised in authoritarian families are obedient and high-achieving but rank lower in happiness, self-esteem, and self-image compared to children raised in less restrictive households. In my case, this type of upbringing helped me to achieve academic and social success, but also led to bouts of depression, anxiety, self-doubt, and limiting beliefs about my ability to control important aspects of my life.

Looking back, I believe that these limiting beliefs first began when my mother remarried and she and my biological father went their separate ways when she, my step-father, sister and I immigrated to Canada. When that happened, my life was turned upside-down. I was separated from my extended family – particularly my maternal grandmother who'd lived with us since my birth – and found myself living in a new nuclear family and new social and cultural environment. This change had profound effects on me emotionally. For example, although I missed my grandmother I had very little contact with her except for the occasional visit over summer vacation. This was the late-1960s and there was no internet, Skype, FaceTime, or long distance calling cards to help keep up regular communication. I deeply felt the loss of this important source of emotional support and my inability to change my situation led to my initial perception that life was something that was beyond my control.

My feelings of powerlessness was compounded by the fact that my biological father dropped out my life completely after we immigrated to Canada. For over forty years I heard nothing from him. He never sent me a single birthday card or Christmas card. He wrote me no letters, gave no gifts, and made no phone calls. I couldn't quite understand how someone who was supposed to love me could simply not even bother to acknowledge my existence. I felt rejected and unloved, and eventually those feeling turned into anger and outright hatred. The feeling of rejection I felt by my father's abandonment was compounded by the fact that in my new nuclear family, I was a step-child. Although my mother and step-father didn't deliberately set out to make me feel different, there were things that happened over several years – both subtle and flagrant – that made me feel insecure and an outsider within my own family.

An additional factor that contributed to my limiting beliefs about my own power stemmed from the things that happened outside my family environment. Very few visible minority immigrants had come to Canada by the 1960s. Most of the immigrants at that time were European and that presented its own challenges for me. For example, although my European neighborhood was safe and friendly, I encountered the occasional instances of racism from other children as I walked to or from school. I wasn't equipped at such a young age to deal with the name-calling given that I'd attended a private preparatory school in Jamaica where I seldom experienced negative interactions with other children, especially about things that I couldn't control such as my skin color. For the most part, I was helpless to change this situation either.

Lessons learned at an early age have staying power. That can be a good or a bad thing because what we learn about ourselves during childhood effects the way we think, feel and behave as adults; often without us realizing it. If, for example, you learned as a child that you have choices and the ability to exert control over your life, then you're likely to mature into an adult who manifests those same traits. You're likely to become an adult with an internal locus of control believing that you have the power to change your life circumstances. People with this mindset direct their lives towards achievement of their goals and take personal responsibility for their successes and their failures. On the other hand, if you learned through experiences that others are more powerful than you and that you have little or no ability to control what happens to you, then you're likely to mature into an adult with fears and limiting beliefs about your own power. You're likely to mature into an adult with an external locus of control believing that things outside of yourself (e.g., luck, fate, or other people) control what happens in your life. People with this mindset tend to leave everything to destiny and resign themselves to having life unfold rather than taking action to make things happen.

Because there were so many things that impacted my thoughts and feelings about my own power in a negative way as a child, I developed an external locus of control. And with that belief and fatalist attitude came other emotions such as depression, anxiety, and anger. Essentially, my experiences had conditioned me to form an unhealthy self-perception which affected my behavior. For the most part, when presented with challenges, I'd tend to fall back on dysfunctional thoughts about my ability to control what was happening. This acted as a limiting belief that created a self-fulfilling prophesy – because I believed that I couldn't control things, I acted in ways to ensure that things remained outside of my control. I'd give up my power and remain passive in situations where if I'd only taken control, I would have seen that the outcome would have changed.

But thankfully there were three major "Aha!" moments in my personal and professional life that taught me how to break through my limiting beliefs and get power and control over my thoughts, feelings and actions. In fact, not only did I learn how to overcome my own limiting beliefs, but the tools I developed allowed me to teach hundreds of others how to overcome their perceived limitations as well. The idea that we put limits on our potential based on our experiences started peculating in my consciousness during my undergraduate studies in experimental psychology. Conditioning rats and pigeons in the lab so that they'd exhibit specific behaviors based on being rewarded or punished for them showed me clearly how attitudes and behaviors are programmed, not only for animals, but for us humans as well. As I worked with these animals, I saw a clear relationship between them and my own conditioning. I saw how my experiences had shaped my perception of what I could and could not control and how this had eventually influenced my behavior. For the first time, I saw how I had been shaped to become the person I was.

My sociology courses compounded this sense of having been programmed by giving me insight into the ways that all individuals are influenced by our family, culture, religion, society, and the world at large. The fact that I was conditioned to think, feel, and behave in certain ways meant that I could be conditioned to think, feel and behave in other ways as well. Just like I'd been conditioned by my experiences, I could re-condition or re-program myself! I could make the conscious decision to change any of the thoughts, feelings or behaviors that didn't serve me and essentially create a version of myself that I wanted. For the first time, I truly believed that I could actually become the confident and powerful woman that I'd only caught glimpses of here and there throughout my life. I saw that I could take control of my mind and behaviors and completely change my life outcomes. This was the first momentous step towards making me the woman that I am today. This concept of self-efficacy (essentially the belief that we are capable of accomplishing whatever we want to achieve based on our own efforts) is necessary for anyone to feel that they have power and control over their life. People with high self-efficacy act on their beliefs and when they take action, their self-esteem, motivation, and self-determination increases significantly. In essence, we're rewarded for stepping out in faith and taking action based on just our beliefs. We create our successes simply by thinking, feeling and acting in ways that are consistent with a success mindset and help to create our failures and disappointments when we set limits on our abilities to control our life.

Another "Aha!" moment occurred while I was a doctoral student and decided to end my marriage. As undergrads we'd been the best of friends but over time the marriage had grown dysfunctional. My needs and concerns were constantly being dismissed and I began to experience significant stress, depression, and anxiety. That sense of learned helplessness that had defined much of my childhood crept up once again because I was unable to control my life in ways that were important to me. No matter what I did to try to change things, things remained the same. But, as the saying goes if you can't change the situation, then you need to change your feelings about the situation or your behavior. In order to deal with my negative emotions I could either accept the disrespect, dishonesty and uncertainty, or I could leave the situation. I chose the latter.

It wasn't an easy decision. I spent years in an ongoing and mind-numbing stay-or-go debate with myself about what to do. I had been taught to honor my commitments and to find solutions to problems. So it felt like I was failing to give up rather than seeing my marriage through to the bitter end. As well, must admit that I was afraid. I'd identified myself as someone's partner for most of my adult life and was filled with fear about who'd I'd be without that role. It took a lot of self-reflection but I shook off the limiting belief that that marriage was as good I could get. I ignored the fact that other people thought that we were the "perfect" couple and would be shocked by the divorce. I took control of my thoughts about the situation, focused on a positive vision of my future, and kept moving forward in the direction of my goals.

Although the divorce opened up a Pandora's Box of financial hardship and broken relationships with some family and friends, it turned out to be one of the best decisions of my life. My emotional well-being improved significantly and the strangulation nightmares that I'd had for years immediately vanished (I later discovered that my subconscious mind had been sending me this specific message for years in an attempt to show me that my marriage was figuratively choking the life out of me). The sense of helplessness and not being able to control my own life had given way to an increased sense of empowerment and self-determination. I redoubled my commitment to not let others put limits on what I could become or what I could achieve. A few years later I met and married the man of my dreams. Now I have kind of marriage that I'd always hoped for. Moving beyond the limitations of a dysfunctional first-marriage opened the door for unlimited joy in my current marriage.

The third "Aha!" moment happened when, after almost 10 years, I left my corporate executive position to start my consulting company *Wired2Succeed Leadership*. To some people my decision seemed foolish. Why would anyone give up the prestige of a corner office and a six-figure salary for the unchartered waters of self-employment? My gut instinct and honed self-knowledge had been telling me that the uneasiness and dissatisfaction that had crept into my professional life was due to the fact that I had begun to feel limited in my work. Although I managed three teams across the country, was responsible for high-priority and high-visibility corporate deliverables, had created best-practices that were embedded into corporate policies, and was sitting on over fourteen corporate committees, I felt unmotivated and disenchanted with my work. Organization-wide restructuring had resulted in changes in corporate roles and responsibilities and I no longer had the time to devote to mentoring and coaching my staff or even engage with them in any meaningful manner. For me, the ability to help people grow and evolve intellectually, personally and professionally was a key intrinsic reward of my work and played a significant role in my self-identify and job satisfaction.

The feeling of being limited and unable to create a working life that reflected my core values began to wear at me. I knew that I had to make a change to remain authentic and be in integrity with what I had envisioned my professional life to be. However, just like ending a marriage, ending a prestigious career isn't something to be done without a lot of thought. Although I was unhappy in a career that was no longer intrinsically rewarding, it was hard to leave behind a six-figure salary. I asked myself whether entrepreneurship could provide me with the material things that I had gotten used to – the designer clothes and shoes; the sport car; the travel, and the prestige of the corner office. I wondered where

I would get the skills that I'd need to launch a company given that no one I knew had done what I was considering. I went back-and-forth with the pros and cons of leaving versus staying. But something within me was driving me; incessantly urging me to venture out on my own and move beyond the limits of my existing career.

Once again, stepping out beyond my perceived limitations paid off. Within two years of leaving my corporate position to start my own business, my net worth had more than doubled. I'd published two best-selling books, and had become an internationally-recognized speaker and leadership coach. I now spend my time doing what I was meant to do; teach people how to overcome perceived limitations, step into their power, and take the lead in their personal and professional life. I live authentically and in harmony with my core values. This positive outcome has yet again verified to me that breaking through limitations is the only way to life a successful and self-determined life.

Whatever your definition of success, it all starts with your sense of who you are and what you're capable of. It starts with your sense of self and your ability to control our own life. It starts with making a conscious decision to break through your limiting beliefs about what you "can't" or "shouldn't" do.

Like all people, the choices you've made so far in your life and all the choices you'll make in the future is based on your sense of self. Your sense of self is the lens through which you view the world and your perception about how much control you have over what happens to you. Your sense of self impacts your decision-making because it taps into your beliefs about what you're capable or not capable of achieving. My limiting beliefs kept me in a state of learned helplessness for much of my early life. My experiences had essentially helped me to develop a habit of passivity – of giving away my power to others.

In order to design and go after what I wanted in life, and take advantage of opportunities that came my way, I needed to develop an internal locus of control. I needed to dig deep and discover my own agency. I had to reprogram myself for success by making the conscious decision to break through boundaries whenever I found myself giving in to limiting beliefs about my ability to control my life. My level of joy, peace and personal fulfillment also increased significantly when I decided to be self-determined rather than letting others determine what I could and couldn't do. Like me, your mind is where you need to begin to make the changes about what you want to see happen in your life. It's where you need to begin to shape your perceptions of yourself to break down the limits you've put on yourself. Living without limitations means breaking down your own internal barriers to success. These barriers are more important than any structural barriers you'll ever face.

Living without limitations is a call to action. It's a call to take personal responsibility for designing your desired future regardless of what's happened in your past. My tests have become my testimonies that I use to encourage people to persevere and create a life of their own design rather than living a "less than" life by default. It's never too late to become the confident, powerful, and self-determined person you were created to be. You have a choice. What will it be?

Jacinth Tracey, BSc, BA, MA, PhD is a Leadership Coach, Corporate Trainer, Speaker, and multiple Best-Selling Author. She left her six-figure executive career to become the CEO of Wired2Succeed. Her mission is to help women optimize their leadership skills and step into their full personal, professional, and financial potential by breaking through glass ceilings, and overcoming fears and limiting beliefs. Her signature W.I.R.E.D Women™ holistic program leverages her doctoral work in mental health and performance management, fifteen years of corporate leadership development, and over twenty years of success coaching across diverse sectors. Jacinth will empower you to create the passionate, profitable, and purpose-driven life of your dreams.

www.wired2succeed.com
https://ca.linkedin.com/in/jacinthtracey

CHAPTER 11   Diana Alli D'Souza

My Vision Pulled Me Through Life's Valleys

My life has been a strange and unplanned journey. So what does this middle-aged retiree say to those in pain, struggling and disheartened?

Accept the journey; accept the wrong turns, the bumpy roads and travelling without a map. Accept the fearful deep valleys; they are part of life's lessons and blessings which occur unexpectedly.

My adolescent and early adult life had thrown me some unfortunate curve balls, and a few real tragedies – including physical, mental and financial abuse from romantic and familial relationships.

My mother – manic depressive, eventually diagnosed as bipolar – left my dad and her three children when I was just ten. We felt totally abandoned. I ran away twice from two homes which I naively thought would keep me safe. One such escape saw me staying with yet another mentally ill relative – this time an abusive aunt in Britain.

Whilst in the UK I learned my adored dad had died as a result of a horrific kitchen fire. Just six months later, I lost my beloved nineteen-year-old brother in a train accident. They both died back in Bombay.

All alone and in black despair, I ended up falling in love with a handsome student from Guyana. This ill-fated romance saw me ensconced in yet another physically and mentally abusive relationship. It was unbearable but back then the laws of the land – and society's disapproval – meant leaving a husband wasn't an option you took lightly. I thought I had hit rock bottom.

Finally with help from my compassionate work colleagues in Toronto, I left this horrific situation. Once again, I ran – but with no women's shelters to depend on and minimal family support, it took months to get through the sexist, antiquated court system to regain custody of my children – along with pittance of child support.

Valleys: deep, dark, hopeless; yet, the valleys turned into blessings. I found myself on higher ground filled with the life-saving knowledge that I was truly in God's hands.

Although many can never get over the anger and hurt life throws them, I feel particularly blessed my descent took these twists because in the end I triumphed.

I forgave those who wounded me through sexism, racism, and violence and been able to finally heal my soul. My pain has helped me identify with those who need me. My valleys have led me to *"my people"* – my tribe of the disenfranchised, the vulnerable, poor, and frightened.

Since my retirement (thirty-eight years *"with distinction"*), I founded www.accessempowermentcouncil.org, which funnels basic necessities, educational tools, and guidance to areas of the Himalayas in India. My journey now sees me marching into South Africa, Guyana, and wherever there is a need. I have received over twenty-five distinguished awards but the biggest accolades are the lives I've helped transform in many communities with success stories and testimonials. When people ask if I'm going to slow down and take it easy, I tell them I'm not ready to kick off my shoes – I am still following God's footprints!

Had it not been for the depths of despair I personally endured, would I be the person I am today, a woman entering her "third chapter" of existence on this planet recognizing the cruelties of life that so many endure? I wonder.

Would I have coordinated a rescue mission to the victims of Hurricane Katrina and other parts of the world if I'd never felt hunger pangs in my own belly? Would I have identified the needs of insecure, confused students at university, and youth in the community who called me *"mom"* for so many years if I had not experienced a life without parental support?

I have shared a small part of myself I have learned to accept life's experiences as gifts, rather than curses. I have taken risks, the Universe opens many doors, some were tough to open, but once in, it has taught me to be relentless and fearless! Gandhi says it best, at least for my personal trajectory: *"Our greatness lies not so much in being able to remake the world as being able to remake ourselves."*

I am grateful for a rewarding, exciting life full of adventure. I have been surrounded in my professional and personal life by both great gurus and colleagues, men and women, who have been generous through mentorship, guidance, and insight. I count my blessings for the little miracles showered on me daily, three beautiful kids, nine terrific grandkids, and the distinctions and accolades received over my tenure. Life needs to be embraced with fulfilment and gratitude!

A whole new me is reflected in the mirror, embracing confidence with great gusto, leader, activist, feminist, advocate, philanthropist, friend, and mentor to many!

Those valleys, how I shudder when I recall them...unforgettable life's lessons providing insurmountable opportunities.

Diana Alli D'souza held many distinguished positions at the Faculty of Medicine (FoM), University of Toronto (UofT) for 38 years. She is the recipient of more than two dozen prestigious awards, an FoM co-recipient, and Aikins esteemed teaching award. She is the recipient of the prestigious Order of Ontario, the 2012 & the Queen Elizabeth II Diamond Jubilee Medal. There are two perpetual awards in her name awarded to medical students, a MD/PhD Canadian, and MD graduation awards. She retired in 2012 and continues her interest in altruism and social responsibility globally through her non-profit Foundation.

www.accessempowermentcouncil.org

VISION TIP   Melody Mbondiah

How To Recognize Your Vision

Sometimes life throws us setbacks that we don't think we can recover from. I want you take in every word I'm going to give you and carefully digest it. Did you know that you are uniquely made for a purpose? Yes, you. Don't think about looking for someone else. I'm simply telling YOU that from today your life will change. All the plans you made will come to life and even if they don't, the fact that you put forth an effort means something better will come up and shock you suddenly. Today is one of those days for your questions to be answered. You won't believe the answers have been locked inside of you. Today you have chosen to hold this book, to read it, and believe what I'm saying, which has YOUR POWER TO CHANGE YOUR WORLD. I want you to experience the power to change the world around you.

This is how my world became awesome in a matter of meeting my destiny. More importantly, I want you to just focus on changing you...yes, don't blame anyone, and don't attach failures to anything or anyone. As you do that, hush and listen to the greatness within you...you hear that, that is belief stirring up in you. You are what you think. Right now, you are setting in motion the purpose for which you were created – to live an abundant life. The people you meet will add flavor to your world no matter how insignificant it may seem. Pay attention because you have a Vision and it's way too great to be unrecognized.

Vision is knowing where you're headed and taking the steps towards that goal no matter how small the steps are. Your vision is your child, your baby. You must watch over it crawling, staggering, walking and finally running. Even though your baby sometimes falls and cries, don't neglect it, check on with it.

Yes, your vision needs "panel beating" at some point. That's not changing it, just making it fit in the here and now. I have done it, so can you. Simply change your mindset and decide what you want, then allow it to come to you. For those who believe, the reason why the crucifixion was at Golgotha – the name means "the place of the skull", is because your battle is in how you think. Change your mindset!

CHAPTER 12   Randall Mitchell

Living My Vision

If today was your last day on planet earth, what would you do? Think about it for a moment. What would you do?

This was the question that was daunting me at the tender age of fourteen. I've always had this aggravating urge to make an immediate impact on others. I'm pretty sure that it came from countless hours of watching motivational teachings and sermons with my Dad, as well as seeing how people's lives change by the words of one man. I promised my Dad that one day I would become a "High-Class International Motivational Speaker." Today, overflowing with gratitude, I can say that I live that dream. I sometimes chuckle at the fact that when we look at successful people, we tend to think that they were born that way. In some cases, there are a privileged few who are born with the "silver spoon & platter." However, for most people blood, sweat, and tears are the ingredients to their success. I usually say that there is a "Story behind your Glory." And as you make your way through my chapter, you'll uncover the hidden story behind my fulfilled dream.

As I write this, I promise that I won't bore you with endless details but share the vital moments which changed the course of my destiny. I also believe that you have reached a critical stage in your development where you are ready to elevate your entire being to the next level of existence. Well, if you follow what I'm about to share with you, progress will be inevitable. So let's begin.

My Dad plays an important role in his community and is quite vocal about the crime and drug abuse that takes place. One Thursday afternoon, as he was on his way home from the church, something terrible happened. He stopped at a four-way intersection, only to find himself being held up at gunpoint by a local thug. Fortunately, my dad was not injured in any way – it was a warning to my dad to stop his anti-gang activity (it *didn't* stop my dad from continuing his mission).

When my dad told us what happened, all I was thinking was that it could have been so different, so much worse, and my dad could've been killed! I told myself that I would try my utmost to no longer take my mom and dad for granted, and appreciate them more.

Why is it that once something life-threatening happens, we start living life with a sense of appreciation and purpose? Another moment that made me feel this way happened a few years back. Our family was not prepared for the news that was about to come.

My mom was diagnosed with cancer. When I heard the news, I immediately thought of death and how I was going to survive without her. On the other hand, when my brother heard the news that night, he ran out the door to buy cake and pop. When he brought the goodies, he said, "Tonight should be a time we celebrate the healing of Mom's body."

That kind of faith is gutsy! That kind of faith says that although it seems as if there's no way out, we will still believe for the best. You might not be facing a drastic problem such as cancer, but there may be an issue in your life where you need to exercise gutsy faith. I'm here to awaken that sleeping Giant within you and invigorate your senses to tackle your situation with Peace & Clarity.

Growing up in a gang-infested, drug-filled community, negative talk was the order of the day. And wanting to become a motivational speaker was the total opposite of what was the norm. I quickly realized that I had to change my vocabulary. I have this personal quote, "If you say you can't, you won't, and if you say you can, you will." I strongly believe that anything is possible once you change your vocabulary. One particular proverb says that the power of life and death lies on your tongue. This means that you can make your dreams come to life by the words you speak. It also means that you can destroy your dreams by the words you speak! Remember that your words can control your thoughts. Therefore, every time you say you can't achieve something, you will begin to believe that you can't achieve it. "So, Randall, you're saying that if I change my words, I will achieve my dreams?" The short answer to that is, Yes! Don't get me wrong, of course you cannot achieve your dreams without hard work and an action plan, but it all starts with the words you use. Change your words, and your thinking will change. And when *that* changes, it influences your actions, resulting in the outcomes you desire. Think about it. When you speak positively, you think positively. And when you think positively, you do positively! As you can see, it all starts with the words you use. Choose them wisely!

This reminds me of the situation I'm in at this point in time. I'm currently in the process of finding the right car for my present lifestyle. I've been searching online, which has been so much more convenient than going out to hundreds of dealerships in colder weather. Every car I have seen comes with the power steering feature, which allows for safer handling when driving.

When I think of a steering wheel, I think of the human tongue. As the steering wheel directs a car, so does your tongue direct your life. Your tongue can either keep you on the right path of life, or it can cause a major accident. Your tongue controls you. Just as a car includes power steering that allows you to drive with ease, the same applies to your tongue. When you speak about your future and where you want to be in the next five years, it should be spoken with great Power. As you direct your life with your words, they should be words filled with confidence and conviction. When you speak with great power, you *turn* and ultimately live with great power. But when you speak with uncertainty, you *turn* and ultimately live with uncertainty. Decide today to speak boldly about your future so you can *power steer* your way through life!

Once my speech was influenced with the right mindset, I knew that I had to surround myself with the right people. Positive People! It is amazing that when you surround yourself with positive people, it's not what they say that lifts you up but what you feel when you're in their presence. It's a light energy that refreshes the soul. And it surely taught me a few things. Let me share this with you.

Everything in life is a choice. What to wear, eat, say, and believe in is all a choice. My dad once said, "Positive people are positive because they choose to be." Believe it or not, your attitude is a choice too. Positive people are positive not because they were born that way or because only good things are happening to them. It's because they have made a conscious decision to be affirmative despite their current situation.

I must admit that it is hard to stay optimistic when things haven't gone the way you intended them to go, but there are a few realities I want to make you aware of.

Firstly, if you don't control your attitude, your environment will. Whenever something bad happens, you most likely become negative, and when things are going well, you're usually happy. It's like being on an unpredictable roller-coaster ride. This is what happens when you allow your environment to control your attitude.

Secondly, you give meaning to everything that happens to you. Whatever occurs in your life has a neutral meaning: you determine whether it's positive or negative. Confident people put a positive meaning to every situation they encounter by searching for the good and focusing entirely on it. Decide today to search for the positive in every situation, and discover the joy of living optimistically!

In regards to having the wrong people in your life, I remember watching wrestling with my dad on a rainy Wednesday evening. One wrestler was being beaten up by other. They were once friends, but were now both in the ring competing for the championship belt. It was hard seeing two friends fighting. It was tough seeing one choking the other and then stretching his arms to just before the point of breaking. It reminds me of what my dad spoke in one of his sermons. He said, "The people in your life will either stretch your vision or choke your dreams." This is quite profound. It is therefore important to surround yourself with individuals who will be supportive and helpful in achieving your goals. On the other hand, friends who give you constructive criticism are not necessarily "bad people". Those are the individuals you should pay close attention to because they love you enough to tell you things others would be too afraid to tell you. Friends who suck the life out of you and drain your energy are the ones you need to be wary of. Watch out, they are either stretching your vision, making it bigger and better, or choking your dream!

One of my pet peeves is, when I hear people talk negatively about other people. My defenses go up because my reasoning is, if they can talk bad about others, they can talk critically about me too! There's a popular saying that goes, "What goes around comes around." With this in mind, I would want you to stay positive when talking about people. I want you to lead by example in your speech. Negative talk is like a virus that starts off small and spreads like wildfire. It is hard to cure unless it is detected and treated in its early stage. There are a couple of things I'd like you to make a mental note of.

The first is to become Aware. Becoming aware means that you are consciously listening to the way you speak to other people.

The second would be to indulge in conversation about other people only if it is positive. The last thing I want you to do is to sugarcoat your words and lie about someone's character just to say something positive. If you have nothing positive to say about someone, don't say anything at all. The gossip virus has to stop and it starts with you!

I've come to realize that what truly makes us happy is when there is progress in our lives, when we feel like we have grown. For example, passing and moving on to the next grade (progressing academically), when you get that promotion at your workplace (progressing financially), when the one you admire finally admits that he or she likes you too (progressing relationally), or when you realize that there is a higher power and experience an unexplainable joy (progressing spiritually). This being said, I want to encourage you to not deviate from your goals once set. I read an interesting quote in my diary last night. "Be like a postage stamp; stick to one thing until you get there." I want you to picture yourself as a stamp that is stuck to your dreams. Never let go!

A fascinating activity I want you to do is to create a Vision Board. Do this by cutting out pictures that best describes your goals and pasting them on a board. Once done, put a postage stamp on each picture. The stamp is there to remind you that your energy should be directed towards achieving your goals. When you look at your board, it will remind you of what your goals are and how devoted you are in achieving them.

I first stepped into the motivational speaking arena when I was teaching the Grade Two Sunday School students at my local church. I was hungry. Not for food but to be able to inspire anybody. And I mean anybody. I was so fortunate to have been able to look after those precious souls. I remember my very first lesson taught: David and Goliath. This is my favorite Bible story of how a little shepherd boy, who was the underdog, slayed a giant. This eventually led him to be king. There is so much we can learn from this story, but I want to point out one particular lesson that I learned. If David killed an ordinary-sized enemy, the story wouldn't have been as significant. For the fact that he killed a giant, he was greatly recognized and rewarded. The bigger the enemy, the bigger the reward. This is where it applies to you and me. The bigger your problem, the bigger your future. The size of your problem is surely an indication of the size of your reward. You might be going through something right now wherein you feel overwhelmed and insignificant. Perfect! This is the precise opportunity for you to change your perspective. Having this attitude, you will face your goliath head-on without any fear. Even if your problem does not get solved, you will have given it your best shot with the right attitude. I don't see how your problem will last with this approach!

At this moment I would like to introduce you to my older brother. He has been a pivotal part in my development as a leader. My brother is quite an inspiring individual. He's a dynamic speaker and is creative with his words. He once told me something that I will never forget. He said, "Failure doesn't mean you will fail there." It was a play on the word failure, as it sounds like fail-here. He further explained that we should look at our fail-heres as temporary setbacks and not as a permanent condition. I told you he was an inspiring individual! We sometimes think that it's the end of the world when our attempt at something is unsuccessful. Failure is only final when you let it be. I think it's safe to say that the person who has never made a mistake has never made anything.

The purpose of my chapter has not been to tell you never make a mistake, but to let you know that when you do, you are one step closer to succeeding. You're never a failure as long as you keep trying. I am reminded by the late Aaliyah, who sang, "If at first you don't succeed, then dust yourself off and try again" (I Care 4 U, 2003). This is the attitude I want you to have. To be able to say, "Although I failed here (present), it doesn't mean I am going to fail there (future).

Now let's be honest, none of us goes out there with the intention to mess up. You get this brilliant idea that will change the world and then muster up all the strength you can find. You get out there, and then unfortunately, somehow you fail. You are baffled at the results because you've put so much passion and enthusiasm into it that you forgot to do one important step, which was to Plan.

Before you tackle any major goal, your first step is to plan. I remember, as a teen, I desired to become an awesome bass guitar player. Every day after school, I would go home, throw my schoolbag under my bed, and sit for hours with my bass guitar. After two weeks, I had mastered my instrument, but when my school report came, I was in trouble, to say the least. My studies suffered because all my attention was on learning the bass guitar. Now I am not advising you to give up something you love and just focus on your studies. However, my advice to you is to plan. If I planned correctly, I would've scheduled certain times of the week for learning the bass guitar and the rest for doing my schoolwork.

Finally, I need you to take a moment to breathe. Breathe in the many thoughts that you have on all that you've just read. I want you to relax knowing that the constant worry of tomorrow is non-existent. All you have is the present moment. As I've become aware of my Words & People around me, so should you. As my life has changed for the Good, so will yours. These two components are not the "be all and all" to your success. However, it has kick started my journey and my desire is that it will kick start you into yours.

Randall Mitchell has been working his entire life with teens, inspiring them to live out their dreams. He was involved in the South African Radio industry for four years as a Radio Presenter and now hosts a lifestyle/magazine show that airs on Rogers TV. His desire is to see that the development of teen character has a solid foundation and has dedicated his life to helping teens take leadership. Randall has risen above the elements and wants to share ways he has overcome them. You can find those keys in his latest book entitled *"TEENERSHIP – Leadership for Teens".*

randallvisionquest@gmail.com

CHAPTER 13   Suzie Hollihan

Loving Life And All It Brings

My life has about making deals with the universe. "If I do this, you can do that" type of thing. I have bargained, pleaded, threatened, and fought for what I wanted in life or for what I thought I wanted. Looking back, many things have not happened that "I willed" because they weren't in my control. The secret for bringing your vision to fruition; it has be your own dream, not anyone else's.

I grew up in a home of mixed ideals: a Mennonite mother and an executive father who was on the road constantly either with work or his hobby racing cars. My mother became an alcoholic and my father left the province with his secretary when I was twelve.

However, I have taken the best lessons from them both and combined them to create a life of creativity and passion. There are lessons to be found in all circumstances we encounter, but you must go through them with your eyes and heart open. Broken relationships taught me the value of being happy alone and an abusive husband taught me to stand up for myself.

Last year I was at odds with my life, crying out for guidance as to the path I should choose next. I have had different careers, from owning a factory with twenty-two employees to running groups for Foster Children who had been abused. I felt there was something lacking, that I was not living to my own life purpose and although I enjoyed each career, I knew it was time to change and that all I had gone through was bundled up in a package to be used for the next challenge.

While driving in the country one day alone, I cried out loud, "God, what I am supposed to be doing? I can do so many things, but what is my true heart's passionate reason for being?" I heard a voice. I could swear it was out loud. Maybe it was, maybe it wasn't, but I heard this, "WRITE! You always wanted to. What can't you just write?"

Now, others may be skeptical, but it doesn't matter. I cried with excitement. Literally. And began writing that afternoon. I figured out how to write a blog, contacted an editor of a local magazine, and he did need help. It was because of that voice I started writing and knowing that it would be my future, and no one could stop me – not even me. Most times we stop ourselves first before anyone else has the chance.

The universe quickly unfolded an opportunity by putting me in touch with a woman who was involved with that same magazine and later in the week we hatched a plan to start our own full color publication. We then waited for the editor who was 2 ½ hours late. Neither one of us had any experience with publishing but thought, "What the heck, if others can do it, so can we. WHY NOT!"

Perhaps it was the "family first" genes from my farm-raised mother and the "competitive genes" from my successful father, but nothing has been able to keep me down. I have staggered and stumbled through bankruptcy, a divorce, a violent relationship, scrounging for food to feed my children, burying my mother and father, and yet I have been able to create a life I love through teaching, writing, and laughing.

I believed in myself for the first time and have now published a book. Opportunities continue to fall in my lap; they may have always been there unnoticed, but maybe I didn't believe strong enough!

It has not been all glory and roses though. I actually had to do the work, and learn, and stumble, and put it out there which is a big hurdle sometimes; to have others judge what you created from your heart. My belief is that anything is possible if it is true to your own self.

And my future is all about sharing what I have learned with the world. I have been able to laugh my way through most everything; there is healing in a giggle. As a community we "live, laugh, and love" as the saying goes and nothing could be truer.

Our little magazine is now across Canada and I have other books awaiting publication.

In five years I shall be retired from my job working with at-risk high school students and writing full time. I know that a foundation has to be built first in order for the "castle" to rise up. It is the challenges that push us ahead and the mindset that anything is truly possible. Instead of asking myself if I can do something, I ask, "Why can't I?"

I have been blessed with four children and six grandchildren and we are all together at least twice a week for dinner or other events. They inspire me to keep going and to share my stories of overcoming those events in my life that could have had me crawl up into a little ball and retreat.

I have always suffered from anxiety and my future vision is to live fearlessly; to stand up in front of a large crowd and yell, "LOVE YOUR LIFE", no matter what. It's yours and yours alone. You are the creator, the producer, and the critic.

But don't be hard on yourself. Look at how far you have come already in life. You are a living, loving being — what more could anyone truly want?

Suzie Hollihan is a dreamer, planner, and doer. She co-owns a bi-monthly magazine, has published books, teaches sewing and quilting, and works as an educator in a program for Youth at Risk. Her many-faceted careers have been in advertising, retail stores, sewing instructor and trainer, owner of a textile factory, and freelance writing. Life is never dull in the Hollihan house! Throw in five children, five of their spouses, six grandkids, as well as a Saint Bernard and you can imagine Sunday night dinners at her house. Her motto: "What a crazy week coming up and I love it!"

hollihan@rogers.com

VISION TIP Dvora Rotenberg

How To Listen To Your Heart

My earliest childhood memories were of not belonging, not feeling connected to the children in school with me, or even with the place that I lived. I did many things throughout the years to feel that connection – to feel a part of rather than apart from. I had low self-esteem and barely any self-confidence. When I thought about myself, I felt as though I just didn't fit in. I tried drugs and was indoctrinated into a cult when I was a teen. They made me feel so connected. I stayed in the cult for many years, married an abusive man, continued my drug use until I knew I needed help, survived mental health issues, and finally one day was able to take control of my life. Once my marriage ended, I began to slowly find myself.

Today I am married to a wonderful man. Although I changed cities and even countries, I feel like I belong here. I feel connected to the place where I live. I have learned many things since moving here.

In 2008 I had the opportunity to visit Uganda. I had never been to a developing country before and it was a life-changing trip. When I returned home, I started a charity and began helping the boys and girls over there. I found that giving of myself to these beautiful children took me away from the chatter in my head and brought me more into my heart and soul. The gift of giving made my heart sing. I started to let go and let my intuition guide me.

I began to wake in the morning with gratitude, knowing that happiness was also a discipline. We choose to be happy. I chose to be happy, I chose gratitude. I practiced being happy and grateful. There is a saying, "Fake it until you make it." Not every day is perfect, but I choose to be happy anyways. I'm not perfect but I work at not being angry and not worrying. I'm compassionate with myself and others. These are my goals.

Listening to your heart is not physical, rather it's following your intuition, opening your mind and soul to the beauty around you, and to the needy of the world. Listening to your heart is to feel; to feel love for others and loving to help them. Listening to your heart makes your soul sing.

CHAPTER 14   Pamela Kunopaskie

Escaping To My Destiny

Sometimes when things are falling apart in our lives they may be actually falling into place.

"Creating a new theory is not like destroying an old barn and erecting a skyscraper in its place. It is rather like climbing a mountain, gaining new and wider views, discovering unexpected connections between our starting points and its rich environment. But the point from which we started out still exists and can be seen, although it appears smaller and forms a tiny part of our broad view gained by the mastery of the obstacles on our adventurous way up." — Albert Einstein

Every once in a while I stumble upon a quote that resonates with, and leaves an imprint on my soul. This quote penned by Albert Einstein was one of them.

Best known for the popular culture equation $E=mc^2$ (which has been dubbed "the world's most famous equation"), Einstein's work won him the 1921 Nobel Prize in Physics which helped in the evolution of the quantum theory.

Always intrigued with two questions, Why? and How?, Einstein has played an instrumental role in the development of over seven theories in his field, all derived from the fact that one theory would not have existed without the other.

So why my fascination with Einstein and this one quote? The first time I came across it, I sat there and reread it over and over. A theory. Wider views, Unexpected Connections. The point from which we started out still exists. Trying to compute how all the dimensions of this quote fit together it finally came to me. If I equated my life to a theory as defined in his quote, then Einstein's words would perfectly define my evolution as a person.

I am not who I was five, even ten years ago, yet the core of who I am still exists. Physically my body has changed with time, but I still have blue eyes, two legs, two arms, and two feet to walk with. I still believe in the golden rule, believe in love, and support the freedom of choice and freewill. However, each one of those emotional muscles has been flexed and has grown with each new connection and experience I have witnessed. I've changed due to the influence of external factors, just as a theory evolves over time due to its external influences, but the premise by which it was conceived remains consistent.

My life has been shaped by millions of intricate connections and similar to a theory, each new connection didn't destroy anything prior to it. Nevertheless each new experience, each new connection built upon the one prior and was needed for me to grow emotionally, spiritually, and mentally. Every experience I've had, the good, the bad, and the downright "ugly", needed to happen for me to evolve as a human.

I once read that the Universe works backwards and that sometimes when things are falling apart in our lives they may be actually falling into place. I believe that ultimately the Universe knows our life's master plan and where we need to end up after it's all said and done. It will provide to us everything we need to fulfill our life's destiny and purpose. For instance, have you ever wanted to be, to do, or to go somewhere, and no matter what you try, and the hurdles you jump to obtain that goal, it seems like it "just isn't meant to be?" At the precise moment in time when you finally give up on the idea, low and behold something better than what you originally wanted comes along with ease and little effort, and most times it happens out of the blue. Why? Because it's part of what you need to evolve and fulfill your purpose.

Like a fine tuned symphony, the Universe will provide all the people, experiences, and things we need to evolve and fulfil whatever calling we may have at the exact time that we are capable of handling it.

All the in-betweens, all the connections that we make are fundamental building blocks that help us evolve and pave way to our soul's purpose. By stating the latter, does that mean I fully understand all the connections and experiences that I have had? Absolutely not! Does that mean that I have consciously learnt something from each connection and experience? Not a chance! Was I saying "Oh thank you Universe" when I lost my job, lost my home, and lost my family all in the matter of three months? Another affirmative. However, all of what I lost made room for more of what I needed. Not always want I wanted, but what I needed at that time.

Every experience that I've had has changed me, and I will never be the same person I was before. The amazing part is that I'm much smarter, more emotionally intact, and far more in tune to who I really am. In order for me to have evolved into this person, the Universe presented me with connections that created the experiences I needed so that change could happen.

Let's rewind to the year 2003. Twelve years ago I was married, had a millionaire's family, two lucrative incomes, a larger than needed house, a pool, high profile friends, yearly family vacations, a healthy bank account, two vehicles, and essentially everything that fit into the societal standard of success. To some, this was the ideal life. But for me, the more I lived it, the further I felt like I was dying. I thought I loved my partner whom I had been with for over fifteen years.

I knew loved my kids and had all the things one should be happy with, but I wasn't. I was miserable.

Unfortunately, I didn't know how to define happiness or what made me satisfied. I just knew that I felt empty, like I wanted to run. I can't count the number of times I would cry myself to sleep knowing that whatever happiness was, I didn't have it. More importantly, after all these years I had forgotten who I was, what I wanted, and was living on cruise control making choices by default.

Now here's the catch. The unhappier I felt, the more I sought after material success to fill the void that existed. New cars, more prestigious job positions, a larger home, expensive clothes – the more I bought, the emptier I felt. I was spiritually dead. I knew I longed for something. My soul pleaded with me to find its fuel, but every earthly fill up station I tried out, left me feeling emptier than before, so to speak.

Something was drastically missing from my life. My deeper self knew it. I now became consciously aware of it, but I could not clearly define what that "it" was that I was missing.

As time seemed to slip away, years passed and the older I got, the more I became driven by my ego. I defined my success from what I had, and tried to embrace the happiness from those possessions which brought temporary happiness. Ninety-nine percent of the choices I made came from a place that didn't resonate with my authentic self (soul), and eventually over time, the consequences of those choices become more and more negative until I no longer wanted to live the "Happily Ever After Story" I had fabricated.

I blamed my husband for my unhappiness, I blamed the lack of time for my misery, I blamed my work, I blamed every possible outlet I could for my despair except for the one vessel that was fully responsible for it...myself.

Each day I woke up feeling trapped. I wanted to run. I wanted to run away so that maybe the internal suffering, the feeling of being suffocated would stop. I had no idea what I wanted in life, but I clearly knew what I didn't want so I created a list which looked something like this:

The Avoid List

- I do not want a job that ties me down.
- I do not want a partner that forgets my birthdays.
- I do not want to have to worry about mowing the lawn every Saturday morning.
- I do not want friends that are needy.
- I do not want to have to schedule every minute of my life.

- I do not want to have to take the same family camping trip to the same park every year.
- I do not want to have to get up early for my job.
- I do not want to feel like I "have" to be intimate with my partner because we are married.
- I do not want to feel guilty for doing things that I love because it doesn't make sense.

...and from this list my search for happiness began.

Equipped with nothing other than a feeling that I was missing out on something and the above list, I set out on my quest to find this happiness thing. I had no road map, no sense of direction, no idea what I was even looking for, but I was adamant that I was going to find fulfillment. I had no plan, but most importantly I had this list and my self-centered ego which was continually looking for the next best thing. So having these two things...it was road to happiness or bust straight ahead!

Not long into my quest I found out that the latter could have not been more wrong. Unfortunately because my motives were ego driven, I started creating connections that would ultimately end a fifteen year marriage and collapse of a lifestyle that I had grown to be very comfortable with. In a matter of months I had given up a marriage, a job, a home, stability for my kids, friends, family; everything that had taken me thirty something years to create was destroyed, and I now had nothing. I had hit rock bottom.

My whole way of thinking, being, and doing had shifted one hundred and eighty degrees. I now had no plans (everything before my quest was scheduled down to the minute); I had goals that varied on my moods,(before I had solid tangible goals that I stuck with), and essentially I floated through life, trying this, experiencing that, travelling, going through multiple jobs, dating many men. You mention it, I probably tried it and yet happiness was nowhere to be found. I was free to be anyone, go anywhere, do anything but I couldn't. I lacked the most essential component – a roadmap for my life written by me, for me, that was given direction from my true self.

Each choice I made had no rhyme or reason, but rather it felt right in the moment. I have always considered myself to be a free spirit at heart, but something felt off and one failure after another started to take a toll on my self-confidence and my motivation to live. The continual rotation of careers, partners, friends, even places I called home blurred my self-identity, and the more "free spirited" I became, the more I began to panic.

What had happened to me? For the first time in my life I was lost. I felt like life had beaten me. I was ready to give up as every choice I made seemed to pull me farther and farther down into a deep hole. I gave up on creating material wealth, I gave up on the notion of being a free spirit, I gave up on making choices because every choice left me feeling emotionally robbed.

I was terrified that I had nothing left to offer, and frightened that I had failed myself, failed my mother...and failed my children. I had hit rock bottom. I remember lying in bed at the end of every day and feeling like I had nothing left to offer anyone and I felt drained. I was emotionally exhausted. I was tired of failing, tired of running... I was tired; tired of being tired.

It was a week before Christmas in 2011 and after a day of going here and doing this and that in preparing for the holiday season, I lay in the darkness and for the first time in years I was smiling. I was thinking about how excited my children would be to open up what little gifts I had bought them with monies I had saved over the year. I was thrilled to be able to go on long winter walks with them and make snow angels. I was elated to attend an evening mass at our local church the night before Christmas. I was smiling from head to toe, and these simple thoughts rekindled a fire that had been smothered by years of self-repression and by simply not being still in my thoughts.

I lay there, watching the snowflakes fall in the moonlight, having nothing, owning nothing, but yet I knew beyond a shadow of a doubt that for the first time in a very long time I had everything that I needed and that everything was going to be okay. The situation that I was in at that moment was not me but rather a result of the poor choices I had made. I wanted and deserved more. It was that night that I decided I wasn't going to be a victim of my circumstances any longer and most importantly, I realized that no matter what had happened to me in the past, I was still here. I was alive. I had fought many battles and had won. It was these battles that now gave me the armor to wear and the strength I needed to start creating the life I was born and destined to live.

That one night in December passed, and for the next three months I went into hibernation. My days consisted of only two things: sleeping and reading. I had always loved books, and they became my new best friends. I frequented used book stores to find literature that would inspire me to be and do more. Thanks to a spiritually enlightened ex, my sacred quest began with the teachings of Buddha.

Book after book I read. I digested, I cried, I wrote notes, I digested, I slept, and I read some more. Day after day I studied books on how to live a life filled with passion, how to be empowered, how to stay focused. With each book researched, I was slowly shedding my old belief system and sowing new values based on finding and honoring my authentic self and letting go of my ego.

The positive reinforcement that I obtained from my readings kept me going. This doesn't mean that all days were good. There were some when I felt emotionally drained. There were others when I wanted to throw in the towel. On those days, it was my kids that kept me going with their warm hugs and heart-felt "I love You's", and a mother that through her own nagging ways kept me pressing forward.

About nine months passed and an amazing thing started to happen. A shift in my being and my mindset was occurring. I was no longer searching for happiness, but now understood that contentment was the result of just being. I had lost every material possession I owned, had nothing other than the love from my two children, and for the first time, life made perfect sense. I knew that "hat" was more than enough.

Depending on the cosmic timing, the state of our being, and our readiness to embrace newness, the Universe seems to know how and when our lives need divine interference. In order to find the essence of my being, I had to shed my old self in order to make room for my new, more authentic self.

My change did not happen overnight, nor did it come without great loss. I suffered more than I celebrated, I cried more than I laughed, but ultimately it was those tears that made me who I am today. Each tear shed lead to me becoming more resilient. Each material possession I gave up made me become more attuned to what I really needed. Each friend I lost made me cherish more those who stayed. Each job I was fired from (and there were many) opened new opportunities for me to find what exactly that I was passionate about. Each old belief that was shattered, cast light onto a new belief that was more in tune to who I was. When I finally had learnt to let go of how I thought life was supposed to be, it was then that new connections, new experiences seemed to magically appear that resonated with my soul.

Every day I am presented with choices and connections that can change my life for the good or the bad. What I do with those connections is entirely up to me. I can sit back and let them pass, or I can fully embrace the opportunity that they present and allow newness into my life knowing that these connections have come at the right time under divine guidance.

It has been almost four years since that snowy night in December and much has happened. I do not live the societal White Picket fence life…and I'm fine with that. My time and energy are focused on those things that make me smile. I spend more money on experiences than I do on things, and I have a career built on my passion that continues to grow. Most importantly, it allows me to have ample time with the people that I love. I am still learning, still evolving, still reading, and now I'm teaching others on how to make the most of every connection they encounter. I have a life plan guided by the real me, and although that the plan may not fall into the traditional lifestyle most people live – I'm okay with that too.

Like Einstein's quote cited; I am a theory in progress. I continue to climb mountains, gain new and wider views, and continue to discover unexpected connections between where I started out and where I am now.

After all that I have seen and experienced, the point from which I started out still exists and can be seen. It just appears smaller and now only forms a tiny part of my broad view gained by the mastery of the obstacles on my adventurous way up.

Pamela Kunopaskie is a Connections Anthropologist, Medium, and Intuitive. She has served as a senior consultant to leading 9-1-1 telecommunications and air traffic control providers, as well as owned and operated three retail chain stores. She has worked with both Provincial and Federal Governments helping small businesses succeed. Pamela taught Marketing, Law, Business Communications, and Human Resources at college level. She has worked for two of Canada's largest retail enterprises, helped guide and connect hundreds of individuals to their authentic self, and traveled extensively throughout North America. Pamela has a plethora of knowledge for business and life.

BIRTHING

THE

VISION

CHAPTER 15   Anita Sechesky

Birthing The Vision

As visionaries, we must "birth our vision" at some point in our lives when we have passionately and fervently desired to bring it forth. I recall times in my life where the struggles were so real, that I would cry out to God asking if this was necessary. Why me? You see, sometimes a vision is deposited into an individual's soul whether it's asked for or not. It can come as an urgency that we must take a hold of and run with or we'd feel the burden and guilt of not allowing it the chance to be birth through us. Another important thing to understand about a direct deposit vision from God of the Universe is that if you do not own your vision, it will be removed from your care and given to someone else who is more than happy to give it the life force it deserves. This is why visions can be so powerful. They're a little sparkle dust from the Universe that's landed on our noses – what are we going to do now? You don't need to have any prior arrangement or acceptance to carry out this role. You were already divinely picked as the most perfect individual to have this honor and responsibility. My days with those past visions that I had birthed seemed as if they would never end. The internal strain and emotional expense it caused me, in hindsight, has always left me with inner strength that I had not recognized in that moment, but as time went by, I discovered the purpose to have experienced what I did.

The birthing of a vision is something that is highly critical to its survival as it needs the dedication, nurturing, and strength to thrive long enough to become established on this earth and not weakened so there's a risk of it being stolen and damaged in any way. Just as a newborn baby is vulnerable before and after birth, so is your vision. The season you enter into breaking ground for your vision, you many find yourself experiencing certain things that are similar to actual childbirth. Here's a list of expectations one must be prepared for and recognize as a natural part of the process to prevent the vision from dying or being stillborn before it's had a chance to inhabit the earth and develop into what it was created for.

1. The false labor you experience will have you feeling overwhelmed and confused because things will fall out of place and you may begin to think or realize that you're not actually prepared to bring this "baby" home and give it the attention it needs to stay strong and healthy. – *Once you see your vision's potential, it's time to accept it for what it is and own it in every sense of the word. This way, you are growing with your vision.*

2. Your support system may let you down. It's very important to never attach a goal to a person, place, or thing. People will always let us down but the true Visionary, the author and creator of the Universe will never do that. Keep your faith strong and your head clear. – *Clarity is the beginning of appreciating this new role and responsibility that comes with it. Allow yourself to breathe and step into this role as a visionary with confidence.*

3. You will experience moments of urgency to get yourself prepared and clear out things that will hinder your attention to your vision. Do it now! There's no time like now to get organized. This will allow you the opportunity to have peace moving forward with no stress from residual responsibilities left behind. This is also the time to make that last check and see where your commitment level is to give your vision the devotion it needs to grow steadily. – *No stress. No clutter of emotions. No unfinished projects left behind. Release what is no longer working to allow time for what is ready to expand in your life.*

4. You start to have cravings for certain things you have avoided for so long, because you desire a familiar taste as you realize something "new" is about to be deposited into your soul, and there's no turning back. Don't do it! Resist the things from the past. Remember, you're no longer going in that direction. That's why you left them behind. It's time to release those desires and quench your thirst and hunger with the things that actually build you up and fatten your vision! Maybe you wanted to get a little extra training that you know will support your vision and never had the time before. Your spirit is telling you to go for it now and get that foundation set up. When your vision is released, you won't have time, just like a new parent. You'll be completely involved and must provide the nourishment and attention it needs to grow strong and healthy. – *You are a maternal soul because you understand the love and devotion to help your vison grow. Take care of you and distance yourself from any critical and negative opinions. This is your baby and you need to protect it from all harm.*

5. As you get closer to the due date, you will feel as though you have carried this vision inside for so long. You're bursting at the seams and you want to see it happen right away. Don't rush it no matter how tempted you are. Instead spend more time in mediation and prayer, quiet reflection, and get your thoughts all together. Prepare yourself for this new responsibility you are about to embark on. You see, it will become something that

requires your focus and determination. If you don't make your vision the priority it needs to be, you may find yourself disappointed and grieving what was given to you. – *You are stronger than you think. Don't ever allow yourself to feel burdened by your vision. Doing so will hurt the vision. It needs all the love and support it can get.*

So many people do everything right, but lose the passion for their vision because they lose their desire, which effects their commitment. There are others who cannot understand the importance of their vision and how precious it really is. You see, a Vision is something that's not about you, it's much bigger because it serves a far greater purpose. The vision that God of the Universe places inside a person's heart will always bear fruit if it is nurtured with love and hope. But if the visionary becomes self-centered and ego-driven, there will be much struggle along the way.

We are energy and everything around us consists of that force. It makes sense that the concept of love is also energy. God is love, and love is the most powerful energy that so many of us freely and openly agree on. Surely we can also understand how the vision from the creator of our beautiful universe is giving us something that also operates on the power and energy of love. It will create shifts in the lives of those who are meant to be in alignment with it.

This is the power of having a vision and I honor you for having yours and bringing it to life. You are a healer and a world changer. You are the kind of visionary the world is waiting for…you are empowered with a vision of love and peace to heal and enlighten so many. Well done!

CHAPTER 16   CJ Mercedes

Visions Of Motherhood

After a series of marriages and divorces by the age of forty-five, I really struggled where I was as a woman, a Christian, and wrestled with some of my belief systems. I didn't want to be a single mom because I believed each child brought into this world deserved to be in a family with two parents that would love and nurture them. I would cry every time a friend or a woman at my church announced she was pregnant or I got an invitation to yet another baby shower. For more than fifteen years I did not attend baby showers…I couldn't deal with my sense of loss and failure.

So after many years in this very sad scenario, I just looked at myself in the mirror and decided that, since this was the ONE life I had, I was going to really strive to create the reality I wanted for my life and my vision. I wasn't going to have the dreams for my life contingent on another person. So single or not…younger or older…if I want to be a mommy, I was going to find a way. I knew, that for myself, leaving this planet without having the experience of mothering at least one child was not an option.

I put out a fleece to speak to God and asked, "If I am to be a mother, then make me a mother. If not, then take this pain and emptiness away from me so I can move on with things." I attended a local fertility clinic a few times and learned that since I was over the age of forty-five, I had less than a 32% chance of having a live birth using my own eggs. I would not only need a sperm donor, but an egg donor as well. I went home, did my research, and soul searched to see if this was the best option for myself. Just because I could do it this way, was this really the right way for me?

After spending much time in prayer, I began to accept that it might not be in my future to be a mom. But, I was still a full and complete woman. I have value and can make wonderful contributions to my community at home and abroad while leaving an amazing legacy. I am perfect just being me. What I really needed even more than becoming a mom was a different way of thinking and seeing the world, and my role in it. Once my mindset shifted, everything started to fall into place.

I began feeling refreshed and revitalized. I sincerely felt I was coming into myself and becoming who I was truly meant to be — a smart, beautiful, vibrant, loving, and valuable woman. Then, after two months of visiting the fertility clinic, going through various tests, and praying about this, the invitation to adopt a baby came in February 2012.

My girlfriend had adopted a baby girl three years earlier from a birth mom who was now pregnant again. I never hesitated, and on May 1ˢᵗ, 2012, my son Stephen was born. There have been some developmental challenges, but nothing overwhelming. He is an amazingly smart, loving, and funny little boy. I am truly blessed. Has the journey been easy? Absolutely not. Has it been worth it? Without a question, Yes. We have gone through a lot together. My son doesn't have Hep-C or HIV, and no evidence of FASD to date. We have just completed other assessments and he's a high-functioning Autistic child with ADHD. We have a steep learning curve ahead of us, but that's okay. Stephen is an amazing little man, and with all that we have put in place for him already, he'll be making huge strides forward. But don't let all of this confidence fool you for a minute…it does feel overwhelming and I do get fearful at times. So I keep taking deep breathes, keep looking up, and affirming the promises that have been given to me through scripture.

Had these events not come into my life, I was prepared to still be a whole person – living my life with full purpose, meaning, and being satisfied with who I am and the path before me. My vision was clear. No regrets – that's an important key.

And the other important key for me was shifting my viewpoint from being a victim. I stopped caring about the social pressures of whether it was right to be a single mom or to be an older single mom; dealing with the stigma of having a career to being on Social Assistance and having a special needs child. I choose to live a life that is genuine and measures up to my true values and not to those imposed on me. Did I meet opposition and criticism from my peers, religious leaders, neighbors, associates, and friends? Yes I did, and I had to not care… this was my life… not theirs, and I had to live it to the fullest. At the end of my life, I want to look back and know without a question of a doubt that I lived authentically and with meaning. The legacy I leave behind will be the one that is fulfilling to my soul. And so can you.

What I realized in my journey is this:

1) God or the Universe's **timing is perfect** – I am better prepared to be a mother now than when I was in my 20's or 30's.
2) That other people's opinions are just that – opinions. They are not my truth. I had to decide for myself what my walk was going to be and if it was contrary to others' approval, then that was fine. It's okay to **live life outside of the "Norm" box.**
3) **Trust…**not just in God, but in myself that I was making the right choices and I was capable to deal with what was coming around the corner.
4) **Affirm** always that we are blessed, and all of our needs will be met on time, or better yet even before we realize there is a need.
5) **Advocate…**it's okay to speak up and ask for what you or your child needs – consider alternative solutions and be relentless with the process.
6) **Self-Care…**when parenting a special needs child, I had to remember to nurture myself. I can only give to my child out of a place of an abundance or

an over flowing cup. An empty vessel is of no use to anyone. Get adequate rest, eat properly, make sure you drink water, and exercise.

7) **Relax and have some fun**...refresh yourself by doing things that reduce your stress which kills more people than many of our top diseases. Revive your spirit by having fun and laughing, and I mean a deep belly laugh.

For me, this was the right path to follow with adopting my son. And I hope to adopt again in the future, but this time I choose older children because they need to be part of a family before they age out of the foster care system.

One more thing I learned is this:

8) **Time doesn't heal all wounds**...what caused us pain five, ten, or twenty years ago can still be as fresh today as when it first happened. What does heal is acknowledgement/ownership and allowing yourself to go through a healing process. Then you can redefine your life and put yourself on a new track in life.

What woman am I? One who has surrendered, healed her brokenness, and embraced all of who she was designed to be. One who is living her life fully and authentically, and at the same time taking on the biggest and most valuable role in her life...being a mommy to an amazing little man. One who is really experiencing and exploring all of what life has to offer. Along the way, I have been blessed with my amazing life partner, Robert, and Stephen with the father he deserves. I am very excited for the future of my family and my visions of motherhood. Let's GO FOR IT! No Regrets!

As my friend Dianna said...this baby may not have come from my womb, but he was made just for me. I truly believe that. Amazing. Grateful.

CJ Mercedes is the creator and executive producer of Family "Norms", "Missionary Life", "Globetrotting with RJ" and launching her own i-TV Network. She is also the radio host of her online radio show FamTalk Radio where she discusses everything to do with family. CJ spends time with projects in Canada and New Zealand, and is the Author of two soon to be released illustrated children's books, *Grandma the PI* in late 2016 and *Three Mommies Made Me* in 2017. When she is not active in her professional pursuits, CJ is happily consumed with her son Stephen and her life partner Robert.

CHAPTER 17   Tanice Marcella

Finding My Authentic Life

I desire a life of helping others in whatever area they need to be supported, whether it be physical, emotional, or spiritual. I have always had a deep burning desire to be of service to others – my one true vision.

Growing up in a small community on the north shore of Lake Superior, there were two types of everything and everyone. Families were either Catholic or Protestant. Families whose parents either worked in the paper mill or were self-employed. Families that lived on one side of the highway or the other. There were older "Mill" homes that all looked the same and newer homes that had an exciting unique flare to them. There was always something that provided a comparable identifier. I lived on the north side of the highway, was Catholic, my father was self-employed, and my mother was the local librarian. We also lived with my grandparents in a mill house, I was the eldest of three girls, and I was always very social. This was my origin, my identity, and the foundation to prepare me for the life that was going to be mine to create.

Reflecting back, none of it sounds out of the ordinary. At the time though, I felt like I was from Mars. My home and family life was good. Really good. We were a tight knit household with this unsaid security "As long as we have each other and always know the truth of who we are, we will be okay." If I came home from school crying because someone had picked on me or whatever sort of thing kids do to each other to hurt their feelings, the message was always the same: it's not true, we know who you really are, and you are loved for who you are and everything is going to be ok. Sounds pretty good doesn't it?

My childhood dream was to travel the world, work with mother, and become a Physical Education (Phys Ed) Teacher. My father was a contractor in the industrial sector and when I was fifteen, I began to work with him as a laborer and equipment operator. The money was fantastic for a young person. I was free to be whoever I wanted to be and had lots of money to go to school, travel, and do whatever else I wanted to do.

As high school graduation approached, it was time to select the career of my dreams. The guidance counselor told me that I would never be able to handle the work load of a Phys Ed Teacher and I should set my aspirations on a more realistic goal. I had already decreased my academic level and didn't have the grades to apply to university anyway. I can remember feeling disappointed and silly. I loved to play sports and although I didn't make first line of any team, I was always good enough to play on them.

All but one of my friends' parents worked in the mill. I wasn't the most popular girl, but hung out with the girls that were. I was always just short of being what I thought was the best. Having been told that I wouldn't succeed with my career goal fit with everything else I felt about myself.

My next choice of profession was to be a Youth Worker, which is exactly what I did. I worked in Group Homes for emotionally disturbed children while I was going to school. During the summers, I would work construction to supplement the poor wage I made in the Group Home. Upon graduation, I headed off to Europe. I never did go back to working in the Group Homes. The money in construction was too good and I loved working with my dad. I traveled during the winters and that took the edge away from living in the small town. For twenty years, construction was my career: work hard all summer and travel for three to four months in the winter. It was good, but I always felt like something was missing. "What I was meant to do with my life is just around the corner," I thought. Mid-way through this career in construction, I decided to go back to school and become a Civil Engineer (I was terrible in math all through high school, but I wanted to be more than a laborer to satisfy my ego). I felt the need to "Be something or someone." Where did that need come from?

Deep down I really wanted to help people, and maybe someday work with Mother Teresa. I hadn't lost that dream. I remember thinking that if I became an engineer, I could possibly work abroad helping in disaster torn countries. That inspiration was in alignment with what felt authentic deep inside, but I never voiced that thought. As for my dream of being a Physical Education Teacher, I never entertained it again. I enjoyed being fit and active, and my favorite pastime was to exercise. However, none of that seemed to translate into a career opportunity.

So off to university I went. During my fourth year of civil engineering, I was sitting in the library studying for an exam on a topic I had grown to deplore. By that point I had missed out on four years of enjoying life. I was thirty-one and I lived and breathed school. My only free time was spent in the gym. There wasn't time for any social life beyond study groups. I was buried in academics and feeling less and less competent as a person with each assignment and exam. I no longer recognized myself and didn't have any clear ideas as to what I would do upon graduation other than go back to construction. So what was the purpose of it all? Why was I chasing a career in engineering if construction was where I would land? There were two things I liked about construction; the money and the hard physical labor. I had no desire to sit at a desk.

One evening, sitting in the library trying to memorize yet one more equation, I fell asleep in the study cubical. I had a dream about myself that I can recall as vividly as though I just had it. I was passionately addressing a group of people, explaining to them how a person really can follow their dreams, how important it was to put their egos aside, and that the whole purpose of life was to be happy and to serve others. In the dream I was desperate about following my dreams. I went on to explain that I had foolishly wasted four years of my life to become an engineer when that was never one of my heart's desires. I woke up confused and burst into tears. I couldn't make sense of the dream or what it meant. I had been working hard and my grades were good. I couldn't entertain the thought that I had chosen the wrong fork in the road. I certainly didn't have the time nor the energy to indulge in such thoughts. I had an exam to study for and chalked the dream up to exhaustion.

It wasn't until 2006 that I finally "came to" in this journey of mine. I had been working on a job in a paper mill. The industry and my life had changed dramatically since I first began in 1980. Not only had I gone to school a couple of times, I was now married and had two wonderful children. People were now constantly worried about the next job as the economy in northern Ontario was beginning to downsize and doors were being closed. I hadn't enjoyed the contract or the work and was grateful it was over. I had been the supervisor on shift and when I walked off the site I knew right then it was the last day I would ever spend on a construction site.

Previously, in the year 2000, I began to take courses in personal training. It was a hobby and an area of deep interest that offset the dissatisfaction of working construction. When I left that job site in October 2006, I didn't know what I would do for work. What was I going to tell my husband? We had just relocated back to the north and we could not afford to maintain our standard of living with just one pay check.

We had been living in Arizona prior to this relocation. While living there, I had the opportunity to work in a Wellness Center and I loved it. I had taken enough courses in fitness that I was able to work as a part-time trainer, assisting people who had been going to physiotherapy, then transitioning into a gym environment. It was the concept of the center that anyone who had been going to physiotherapy, cardiac rehab, or some form of occupation therapy were already in the routine of going out to exercise and needed to make it a permanent part of their wellness lifestyle. The philosophy resonated with me and I thoroughly enjoyed the work.

When I was driving home that fateful day in October 2006, it hit me hard. I wanted to be a personal trainer, nutrition and life coach. It sounded crazy. I didn't even know if such a job existed and where on earth was I going to find work doing that? How am I going to explain this to my husband, family, and friends?

I could see myself helping people and encouraging them to reach their goals of getting healthy. There was a new facility that had recently opened the year before we moved to this community. It looked stunning on the outside. It was massive and I could see myself driving up to the building and going to work there. I could see myself smiling and happy. I had never voiced that I wanted a complete career change in the past. In fact, I had never even voiced it to myself. Fitness was always just a hobby.

When I discussed my goal to change my career with my husband he was not surprised. He was supportive and said that I absolutely had to give it a try. I could always return to construction if it didn't work out. As for our lifestyle, we would have to adjust it accordingly. That was my green light. The rest was up to me.

I had to write a resume. All of the experience I considered to be of any value in my life was not related to the fitness industry. My only experience had been in the Wellness Center and I wasn't sure if that would qualify me for the job I was applying for. It had been too much fun and enjoyable to qualify as work.

I only wanted to work at the new gym with the glass front wall. The "fitness palace" is what I considered it to be. Working anywhere else was not an option. If I was going to chase this dream, I was going to really go for it. The more I worked on my resume the more I realized that I was qualified for the position of a personal trainer. I held fast to the vision that I would succeed and began to feel authentic in my goal.

I applied and got the job. I have been working at the same facility for eight years now. I have never worked at any other job for more than six months. I have continued to further my knowledge base and education in the health and wellness industry annually. Every accreditation I study for feels as natural as reading a great novel. It doesn't feel like work. I have days that I wake up and feel tired and would love to go back to sleep, but I never have days where I wake up and dread going to work. Interestingly enough, the only challenge I have ever faced with my new career is a personality conflict with a supervisor. It was a conflict larger than any other I had ever faced in all those years of construction and working predominantly with men. However, the conflict was one with great wisdom in it. Through the process of resolution I held the person in love, because I knew that this person was caring individual. I also knew that I was exactly where I was meant to be and I couldn't envision myself working anywhere else. Through love, personal detachment, and a deliberate resolution process we were able to resolve our misconceptions of each other. To this day, we continue to work together and support each other in what we do. If I had not held fast to my vision, I'm certain there would have been a much different outcome.

Being in alignment with my dreams and values in my career has given me the fortitude to confront any potential derailing projections that cater to my insecurities. I spend each work day helping people overcome obstacles they thought were impossible and it leaves me feeling honored to be in their lives. It never feels like work. It's always fun and very enriching. With each client I find new goals and new areas of interest I want to learn about.

There have been many obstacles along the way, but I have come to learn and understand that all obstacles are of my own creation – my own self-imposed limitations. I am blessed to have had an origin that was not influenced by any life altering traumas. Any emotional or spiritual roadblocks I have had or come across are dealt with head on using the plentiful resources that are available to every one of us. Follow my heart's desire for this life is what really matters. That feeling of waiting for everything to get better before my life gets better hasn't existed since I began my new career eight years ago. There have been many tools, experiences, and people who have influenced this journey. My most precious gift is time. I have a sense of urgency to get all the love and enjoyment I can extract out of each day. I no longer allow people, places, or things to occupy my time that leave me feeling anything but love and joy. This is not to say that I don't have challenging days because I do. However, I set the intention to make it the best day of my life, and to love and serve as many people as I can. It might be the final moments of my life so I better make the most of it.

We live in such a decadent society. I could have easily been born in an impoverished village in India or Africa. I have traveled to countries where the bookstores don't have a self-help section. How fortunate am I to be born in a country that can indulge in self-help. I don't have any family members who have been lost to the devastation of war. I truly have been born privileged as a white Canadian person. I have never had to deal with discrimination and my birth place has determined that I will live and not die of starvation or an illness as avoidable as malaria.

It takes constant vigilance to be in a position of gratitude and good health of mind, body, and spirit. However, the awareness is well rewarded. There have been many masters who have walked before me and have documented their experiences. I don't have to rewrite history to live my best life. I just need to learn from others and follow my heart. When my vision gets cloudy, I reach out for help to those who are looking on with fresh eyes and the wisdom to help me decipher where to place my foot next. It is through the courage of reaching out that the reward of recovery from any difficult situation is granted.

My intentions are my roadmap for action, and my actions create my reality. I like who I am. In fact there isn't anyone else I would rather be.

Tanice Marcella originally studied civil engineering and worked the field of civil construction for twenty years before feeling the need to switch careers and live a life of health, fitness, and well-being. As a Life Coach and Certified Personal Trainer together with certifications in nutrition, yoga and meditation, Tanice is able to help you map out a path that will eliminate the obstacles that stop you from achieving the healthy lifestyle you desire. Tanice lives in Thunder Bay, Ontario, on the shores of Lake Superior enjoying the majesty of nature in this part of Canada.

www.tanicemarcella.com
tanmdelsol@gmail.com

VISION TIP   Saskia Jennings-de Quaasteniet

How To Be Courageous

"You can't do it alone, and you have to do the work" Werner Erhard

As a woman in her early 40's and living the good life, I wasn't prepared for the day when I realized in fact my life had become boring and routine. I expected that at my age, I'd be living a life full of freedom and joy. I suddenly started feeling trapped, frustrated, overwhelmed and depressed. I had totally lost my bliss!

My *midlife crisis* actually made me really sick and I learned a few hard lessons, although I never recognized that I was in crisis mode.

The biggest breakthrough came when I gained awareness about the connection of my mind, body, and soul. I learned to listen and accept my body's signals and most importantly, how <u>not</u> to ignore them. Now I wake up every morning with the thought that something exciting is going to happen.

Do you know? It is women in midlife who will transform human society. All it requires is that you put yourself first: self-acceptance is the foundation of creating a fulfilling life. It helps you to sharpen your focus on your goals and dreams, small and big. It starts with listening to your own heart and it takes courage to do that. It's a learning curve and part of your journey. Take the time to listen, and start with asking yourself simple questions. Listen to your own answers and take one step at a time.

Know that you can trust yourself. You have all the power within you. Become a master over your own physical, emotional, and mental health and turn your midlife crisis into a state of creativity. The more clarity you gain, the more you can answer your own questions: what do I want, and how do I create my life that's full of vibrancy?

There's a powerful message in Werner Erhard's quote. When you want to take on your journey into harmony and vitality, find the expert & professional who can help you.

You create transformation and move forward much faster with an accountability partner. Seek the support of a coach or mentor, work together with a therapist.

Now think for a moment: how would that change YOUR life? What impact would you make in the world?

You have a choice… investing in yourself is "minimum risk & big return." Be well.

CHAPTER 18   Matthew Finch

Journey Through A Radical MindShift

It Starts With a Question - From the age of nineteen, I began to think about strange things. At the time I believed they were common thoughts that every nineteen-year-old would have, but as I found out later these subjects were rarely thought about by others in my life. Even though I would do the common things that a teenager would do, a feeling told me things were vastly different than what I was participating in at the time. I remember one particular occasion playing beer pong at my friend's house late into the evening and suddenly, without hesitation, my mind wondered to a place of contemplation, focusing on the importance of being mindful that the power of choice corresponded with each and every experience you lived. I would also get lost in the concept of language and how vocabulary plays an important role in creating reality. It wouldn't stop there. I would experience thoughts of how emotions can be a communication device to connect with   something much greater than one's self. This didn't make much sense to me at the time nor did I completely trust what I was thinking about, but something within me, perhaps a voice, told me to keep exploring these "random thoughts." So that's exactly what I did.

The yearning to explore these thoughts led me to ask some very profound questions. What is the power of choice? Why be mindful of my communication? How does emotion help me to connect to something greater? Although I didn't fully understand these questions mentally, and I had no idea how to connect with them emotionally, I was nonetheless eager to experience them in way that would allow me to become more intimate with them. After all, I knew that the power of imagination and questioning would lead me to develop a belief system that would engage me to seek something that I didn't have access to. In other words, exploring information that I didn't know.

I felt compelled to pursue these endeavors to bring insight into such questions. However I didn't know this undertaking would result in a culmination of experiences that eventually led to an experiment of exponential importance. For the first time, I am writing my personal account of my eleven year experiment. My hope with this chapter is to outline the challenges I faced in order to be where I am today. My intention is to provide but a speck of inspiration and realization that everything you go through in life is important and contributes to your personal success. We both know that if we begin to realize the importance of our triumphs by embracing our authenticity, then we can ultimately find a place of sustainable happiness. So let's explore our authenticity together.

Service the Pain - This experiment changed my life forever. But this was not just any experiment. From the very beginning it had no forcible end nor did it have a clear vision of tangible results to reach. This experiment was instead a focus of what it would be like to learn or remember NOT the art of conceptual servicing another human being, but being what I consider a holistic state of service by learning how to help myself. Knowing how to truly take care of me. Examining and evaluating the underlying truth in why I would react to things and the fundamental reasons my behavior would be a certain way. I knew this form of holistic service would require complete integration of the all the bodies: mental, physical, emotional, and spiritual. Interestingly, most of us embark on this particular experiment whether we are conscious of it or not. The results depend on if we choose to embrace such an experiment by preventing ourselves to not abandon it or attempt to seek something else other than the experiment.

I noticed that I was conscious of this at an early age and I wanted to take advantage of it. So what I decided to do was create an intention to have an experience or experiment that challenged me to, not only learn how to say the right thing, but be the right thing as I participated in daily activity. I also wanted to learn more about these concepts, which I mentioned early in the chapter. This desire, to create a type of intention, provided an experiment eventually directing me on a series of experiences that resulted with me getting a job in the service industry. When I was hired by a well-known coffee establishment on June 10th, 2004, it allowed me to open up to a realm of information I didn't otherwise have access to. Little did I know at the time that this particular position would transform into an eleven year experiment entailing many adventures which created profound learning opportunities.

The eleven years with my employer had many challenges and adventures. During the time of great challenge I could have, on several occasions, chosen to abandon the experiment and create a different experience that would have made me "happy." I place that word in quotations because deep down I knew the abandonment of this experiment to pursue more ego driven desires would only serve my happiness on a temporary basis. So instead, I chose to continue. As I worked, people viewed me as a person that only served coffee. In the service industry most people, without knowing it, project their conflicts onto you and place blame for their issues. Because we serve coffee and tea, which is an important must have for the work force, people come in slightly overwhelmed and stressed. By allowing myself to be in such an environment and subjected to these behaviors, I was able to learn more about not only my own emotional wounds but understand why people carried their wounds. This allowed me to develop levels of compassion, patience, and authenticity. It also allowed me to face an array of spiritual challenges. Sometimes the challenges would force me to try to change my circumstances but all attempts failed because my spirit wanted to complete what was not yet finished. My frugal attempts in applying to hundreds of jobs, starting and failing multiple businesses, and studying numerous subjects produced little to no tangible results. So I continued to do independent research to find what my passion was while learning more and more about humans and how to serve them.

I spent the majority of the eleven years studying some sort of formal education attempting to try to figure out how I could apply the knowledge and wisdom I was accumulating at the time. From studying botany and landscape architecture to holistic medicine and metaphysics, I was on a mission to find the right thing to help people and at the same time make money doing it. Meanwhile, as the years progressed, I was increasingly faced with oppositions from my mental and emotional state. I became bitter and angry that I was still working at the same place, knowing I could be doing something much greater. At times, my resistance was so great that I would find myself in the shower at the end of the day crying about why I had chosen to experience something that would be so painful. To limit myself to a service job when I knew I could be doing something much greater and with a different level of impact. I didn't realize at the time that what I was doing was exactly what I was supposed to be doing. The experience was providing the foundation for something greater in my life.

It was my tenth year into the experiment, and I remember a specific experience that would forever change my mindset and approach. I had to work one evening and as the shift manager, I was responsible for customer support, and all of the closing procedures including cleaning, food and beverage prep, inventory, and money. I remember walking in after a long day of school and examining the store from port to stern. It's what I did. I had to have control over every aspect of operations. After all I was the manager. I examined the store, and the more I examined it, the more I upset I became. Nothing was done. The lobby was dirty, prep was not done, dishes were piling up in the back, and the pull wasn't done. The pull is taking the pastries out of freezer and placing them on the shelf to thaw for the next morning. It's a series of tasks that if left undone, I was responsible to complete as well as counting inventory and tracking the numbers. That takes about an hour, which I didn't have that night. When it was time for me to pull the pastries, I had enough. For several hours I had been running around trying to complete what the day shift had failed to do. I was in the back of the store when I became overwhelmed, punched the freezer and asked myself, "Why the "bleep" am I still here?!" I was upset, which was a rare occurrence for me in the first place. I remember almost crying when my co-worker walked in the back and ask me what was wrong. I told her what was going on and I specifically remember what she said that change my approach, moving forward. She told me, "You know who you are and where you're going. This is temporary, so make the best of it. You're a great guy with a huge heart, many people will soon recognize this, and everything that you want to do in the future you will accomplish." The impact of her words allowed me to tap into my spirit and I was transformed forever. I was now okay with where I was, and I became mindful of when I was trying to manage things beyond my control. At that moment I let go of urge to get out of my situation and instead started embracing it. A year later I was ready to embrace something more.

It was May 10th, 2015. A Sunday afternoon shift and everything was as normal as could be. Sundays are the days of the Frappuccino. Families come in and their drink of choice is my specialty. I was on bar making those drinks when a thought that I hadn't contemplated in quite some time emerged into my awareness. A voice told me it was time to quit. It was time to put in my notice. I began to question it. What about my finances, my benefits, and my stock options? I would lose it all. Interestingly, as I reviewed this in my mind I was okay with the loss because somehow that voice was telling me that it was time to leave and everything would be okay. Interestingly, five minutes after I chose to follow the voice, I went in the back to get ice and one of my coworkers ask me the question, "Matt, when are you going to quit?" I smiled and replied, "Well I just made the choice now." So that day I put in my thirty day notice. My last day was on June 10th, 2015, my exact hiring date. A complete eleven years. I hadn't planned for the dates to work out that way. I took it as a sign that everything was exactly as it should be and I was on the right track.

Let's Get Real - One of the most influential outcomes from the experiment was my learned ability to convey the uniqueness of my personal authenticity. The capacity to continue to develop and maintain personal authenticity is a journey that doesn't end, which may disappoint most people since by nature we like to arrive at a destination. I choose to use the term "being authentic" in the context of owning the ability to be honest and truthful to my thoughts, emotions, and actions by embodying a state of self-awareness, self-responsibility, reflective dialogue, and integrity. This state of genuineness is often spoken about but rarely practiced. During my eleven years of service, I observed that few people practice authenticity, and I say this without judgement. I discovered that being real creates a strong presence in all that we do. Unknowingly, it commands respect from all we encounter, and demonstrates a deep level of compassion and love for others. Authenticity lives within our life's process without reaching a specific destination.

So how did I strive to reach authenticity when I trembled with the notion that it appeared to be impossible to reach an end result of what my view of authenticity looked like? The very quest for this conclusion is perhaps what was impeding my growth in the first place.

I have learned that how I behaved, my traits, qualities, attributes, and even my values stem from the core of my ego. The development of these characteristics allowed me to become aware of what I was honest and dishonest with in my life. This relationship encompassed the parts of myself that were both genuine and inauthentic. Being aware of this conflicting relationship within myself allowed me to observe how it played a role in my imperfections and associated behaviors. The more I focused attention to this relationship, the more I became powerful in combating my reactions to things. Now I can create a way to discover from the present moment and then take action from my place of discovery.

One of my favorite inspirations is B.J. Yacobi. He once said, *"If the quest for personal authenticity is just for self-fulfillment or self-actualization, or for the gratification of personal desires, then it is individualistic and ego-based. However, if it is accompanied with the full awareness of the others and if it is integrated with all the aspects of the outside world, then it is a worthwhile strive and not a superficial trend."* – B.J Yacobi. He showed me that we have the power to be responsible for who we are as it relates to our personal authenticity. He also showed me the importance in using our authenticity from a place of serving others and not just ourselves. I learned that we create these challenges. We get caught up in the gimmicks of putting forth a facade to avoid looking bad and strive in looking good. We cover up our natural gifts, which makes up who we are, and instead settle for such gimmicks to gain acceptance, attention, and validation for what we are not.

My solution to this challenge is quite simple: the possibility of acknowledging that it is impossible to maintain a state of indefinite authenticity. This is but a declaration I made, on a continued basis, in order to achieve a higher state of legitimacy. Why did I do this? Think about the natural cycle of a day. The sun climbs each and every morning which gives rise to the day. When the sun sets, it allows the prevailing darkness of the night. This cycle of light and dark permeates every day for as long as we have known it. Like the daily cycle and pattern of the light and darkness, our minds work in a very similar way when it comes to the construct of it embodying the states of authenticity/inauthenticity. The light and darkness of the day must coexist separately as well as together in harmony to complete the cycle of a day. The same must go for our authentic parts as well as the inauthentic ones.

What Now? - Learning this valuable lesson of genuineness, I began to discover who I was and what I was doing. My vision become clear and my direction was being created right in front of my eyes. I was confident and determined to create yet another experiment, however this time it would be in the form of allowing me to obtain what I desired most and importantly, I was ready to receive it.

Now I have three startup companies that align with my trajectory in life. Two of them entail marketing and the other is a coaching and mentoring business focused on allowing people to access the necessary emotional and spiritual framework to create an intentional life. My fundamental skills, talents, and values are now being leverage in way to create something of my own that will service people to allow them to create what they want in their lives.

My Message - The trend today is working towards getting out of what we have to do to satisfy our financial success and succeed by doing what we want to do so we can create personal success. But often it can be challenging for us because deep down we wonder if we are worthy enough to do what we want so we can be happy. Imagine the discovery of tuning into what and who you are by realizing the power of authentically knowing yourself. Imagine if you transformed what you are currently doing into an opportunity to grow and learn about who you are. Knowing who you are, you can recognize the parts of yourself that you love and hate. Once you know this, you can take ownership and begin to process on what it is you detest. By releasing the overwhelming elements that you abhor, you can reclaim your power and start to feel a level of confidence you didn't have before. The trend you intend to provide will now read to your family members, clients, team members, and co-workers. This trend offers an unconventional approach that entails one simple thing, yourself. Just remember these three words, "Just be yourself" and you will be ahead of the game in everything you do.

Matthew Finch is a certified Life and Career Coach, Reiki Practitioner, and is pursuing a Metaphysics Doctorate. His start-up companies focuses on solving personal and professional problems. Matthew not only inspires individuals through authentic, real-life team experiences that strategizes, coordinates, and implements personal and professional transformation, but coaches, mentors, and facilitates success.

https://www.linkedin.com/in/intuitiveglobalcoach
www.intuitiveglobalcoach.com

VISION TIP   Barbara Jasper

How To "Mom" Without A Manual

Funny; isn't it? Babies don't come with instructions, but every family has a vision to be normal. We wing it from day one. Oh boy, do we wing it! Becoming a mom at age twenty-three, I had NO idea what I was getting into. I thought having kids - lots of kids - would be *fun*. Please... stop laughing; I really did!

Fun. Yeah, right. Fun is not being at the hospital with three sick children for the third time in the same number of months. Into the Emergency Department I walked, and said, "I think my child swallowed a bottle of pills." Thirty seconds later I found myself and three kids quarantined for hours. My eldest was four and had chicken pox (and apparently you can't bring a child who is sick to a hospital when one of your other children might be dying!) Who knew? My youngest (who was one) had hand, foot, and mouth disease (which apparently is also contagious), and the middle one (who was three), well...she decided to break into a bottle of Children's Acetaminophen and swallow every last pill left in the bottle. Don't ask me how she got through the childproof lid – and before you judge me, know that the bottle was locked closed and high up on a shelf well out of reach. If the Olympics had baby events, my kids would be Gold-Medal Champs! *"Mom, Jess has purple juice in her mouth!"* is something I'll never forget. After a charcoal treatment with a nurse who wore more than my daughter drank, and a stern talking to, I was released on my own recognizance. FINALLY able to go home and realize there's no perfect vision when it comes to family life.

Being a mother has been one of the most unique, rewarding, and exhaustive experiences of my life. I went in blind, having absolutely no experience and I did a pretty great job. Even my toaster came with a user manual. It hasn't always been tough though. We've had amazing family experiences, and playing and breaking the rules has been fun. Hey – I'm the Mom, and I get to say, "My family, my rules, even if we break them in the end."

Now that my kids are grown, I'm getting feedback that I've been an "Awesome Mom". Listen, learn, play, forgive, love, apologize, trust, be grateful, and be kind: this list is their reasons why. I live by those words, and I encourage you to as well. Being a parent is a gift – the biggest one you'll ever get. Your vision grows with your family. Don't take it for granted... Ever!

CHAPTER 19   Stephanie Leivas

Passion And Destiny Collide

As I look back at my life seven years ago, three months after my second husband walked out on me and my two children, I had to sit and ask myself, "What went wrong? Where did this all start? How did I get where I'm at now?" I was abandoned and very ill with something I did not know but had a pretty good idea what the illness was. I pondered all the questions that flooded my mind like a raging river. "Why? How?"...and everything in between.

I did a review of my whole life and all the answers started to come to me like a whirlwind of the choices I had made that just pushed the passion of my soul so deep down it was almost unrecognizable.

For the first time, I admitted to myself that I could read people's energies and I was extremely good at knowing when something was very wrong. For instance, two weeks after leaving Arizona, where I grew up, and moved to Virginia with my husband, I knew I should have packed my bags and headed back to Arizona, but I didn't. You need to trust your intuition because wrong choices will eventually catch up with you. Intuition is your life's GPS and it never steers your wrong.

I believe that most of the choices I made were not the Oxygen for my Soul, which was following my passion. The consequences of my choices caught up with me in the form of being diagnosed with Multiple Sclerosis as a result of ongoing sacrifices, and giving my power away. I did this continually for acceptance and love, again and again.

I learned about relinquishment, abandonment, scarcity, fear, guilt and judgement through my journey. It was all unfolding to what my life's purpose was, and to be brutally honest to myself, what I had done was to misalign myself with the Divine.

I had an awareness of Quantum Physics and my Guides directed me to gather extensive information on New Age scientists and motivational coaches. I became a Master Reiki Master with three Reiki Master Certificates: Uski, Tibetan, and Chakra.

I learned how powerful our minds really are. You need to get your heart and your mind in alignment. Your heart has an energy field that's actually been proven by science and is connected with everyone and everything on this earth. When this happens and you act, "As If" then you tap into the Truth that your Soul knows and is a part of the Divine.

My passion was coming into sync with my destiny. I started to do Psychic readings and then became an instructor at the Americana Leadership College. I became fully conscious that every time in that moment you have a choice to either be in alignment and do what your heart desires, or don't. This is what chips away at your very being.

Passion is the oxygen to the soul. I knew this since I was three-years-old but I continued to go against my soul's vision and do what everyone else wanted or what I was told to do.

Now when my purpose and destiny collided, everything was laid out right in front of me on a silver platter. It was like the Universe was saying, "Now that you know how energy works, and how powerful your mind is, go out into the world and teach people how to be in alignment with their own soul's purpose and vision. And what will happen if you don't?"

That very moment is when I decided to open up to the possibilities. Who could I help? How would it affect their lives?

When I decided to move back to Arizona and be around my family, it was not what I had expected. More lessons and more decisions I had to make but with more experience and wisdom behind me.

After living in Arizona for two years, my daughter and I decided to move to Las Vegas. I also was guided very strongly to take one more huge step in my Spiritual Journey. It was to learn how to read the Akashic Records. But then my guides took me even further and lead me to an amazing lady who taught me Soul Realignment with the Akashic Records. Finally, my destiny was part of my vision.

I took all three of her courses and became an Advanced Soul Realignment Psychic. Now, I am truly living my passion, helping other people realign their purpose and soul journey to healing, showing them where the misalignment happened, and in what life time. Now, my passion and destiny are now in sync.

Stephanie Leivas grew up in Parker, Arizona. She became a Reiki Master, then an Ushi, Tibetan and Ckakra Reiki Master. Stephanie has actively held Psychic readings and Psychic parties. She took classes from the Americana Leadership College on how to connect with your Angels and Guides, became an instructor there. She learned how to read the Akashic Records. Stephanie is now a very successful Advanced Soul Realignment Akashic Records Psychic and lives in Las Vegas, Nevada, with her daughter and son.

www.akashic-alignment.com

VISION TIP   Yonnette Kennedy

How I Found My Peace In Chaos

Life without Peace - My life without peace was living in a dungeon of doom feeling extremely tormented, causing great physical, mental stress, makes me feel possessed by excessive force of darkness, all burdened down with the cares of life, digging into every opportunity but I find no peace, without peace I was very discontented, seeking the things of the world, which is temporal with an attitude of greed and selflessness chasing after endless rainbows and I never find satisfaction.

As my desire grows for more, I become very destructive to myself and others. Lack of peace leads to stress, depression, anxiety and fear. It makes me feel there was no hope, it could lead to suicide. The only way out of this tragic lifestyle is to seek God who gives peace. Material things cannot satisfy the desire for peace.

Peace brings contentment - Peace brings contentment to the heart, soul and mind which lead to spiritual uplift. As I begin to grow in my spiritual walk, there is a manifestation of God's peace within and around me, and Persons become attracted to the peace of God in me. When we walk in God's peace, we walk with his divine favor and the fullness of his blessing leads to prosperity, spiritually, physically, mentally and emotionally.

God's peace is like a fresh wind passes over a field of dry trees, as the wind moves, we see the trees begin to spring fresh leaves and blossom, which brings forth fruits. Peace is contagious, it change an entire environment. You feel it in the atmosphere, the peace of God is our source of strength. It brings healing to the body, soul and mind, is the best medication for your entire well-being. It helps to prevent chronic diseases, and you will live a long and healthy life.

Peace doesn't always mean the problem is over. It can bring that sense of satisfaction even in trying time, knowing that God works all things good for those who love and serve him. When I begin to understand the magnitude of God's love for me by sending his son Jesus to die for my sins, it brings me peace. The more you seek God there is a full revelation of his peace. Peace is not an object that can be seen, but it is a presence that human words cannot explain. It is a beautiful, sweet experience.

CHAPTER 20   Andrea Lavallee

Living My Empowered Life

A better life is what I always wanted for myself and my family. This all started when I discovered that I was a mompreneur. I didn't know it then, but I sure do know my true life calling now. I attempted everything I could to find financial freedom. I was involved with the majority of the network marketing businesses that seemed to be a good fit, but nothing worked. I wasted a lot of effort, time, and money. However, I am very thankful that I tried. One day, I decided to meet up with a friend for lunch. We chatted about her wanting me to join her business venture. I completely trusted her, but I couldn't see myself joining another network marking company. I wanted to, for once, stay focused on myself and put all my energy into building my current business. As I started to tell her my stories of all the companies I had enthusiastically signed up for, which ultimately ended in defeat, I started to cry out of the frustration these experiences had caused. I had not recognized that all the failures had disappointed me so deeply and these feelings had stayed with me all these years. All of a sudden, she mentioned something I never realized I was doing. She said, "You might have failed, but you never quit. You kept on persevering through all the failures." I was enlightened to the fact that she was right. While I definitely never quit, I kept going and continued searching for my work-life passions.

I learned that the network marketing era was not a huge loss for me. I found that one needs to have a strong focus if one wants to get anywhere in business, and you cannot do that without having passion. I realized I had no passion for those ventures. Fast forward a few months and another network marketer was trying to recruit me, so I told him it looked and sounded great but I must admit I just didn't have any passion for it. He replied, "You don't need passion to do this." I chuckled to myself as I finally recognized that without the right desire, I was going to be wasting my time. But what was my passion? What did I stand for?

It all started when I was in my 40's, my husband was in his 50's, and our son was four. I realized that I was forced to do it all. About three years after returning from maternity leave, I was completely drained. I knew it was time to start finding my purpose and living my dream so that I could have more time for my family and myself.

I had a very stressful, highly demanding job. I had a son who needed a lot of my attention and extra loving care. I had a husband with chronic back pain who did not drive in the city, and we had no family close by to lend a helping hand. A typical day for me started by dropping my son off at school by 7:30 in the morning, followed by catching the train downtown, and then picking my son up after finishing work.

Afterwards, I was coming home to make dinner, giving my son his bath, and putting him to bed. However, my day was not over yet because I would stay up past midnight in order to get work done. Somewhere in my full day, I needed to buy groceries and run other errands. On the weekends, I would take my son out so that he was not spending all his time in front of the TV. After returning from a fun and exhausting day, I would start working on assignments for my business before starting dinner. If my husband helped one day with our son's bath and story time, he might not be able to help the next day due to pain and exhaustion from his back issues flaring up or by working his physically demanding job. After being a solo parent for three years, I just couldn't do it anymore. I realized that I had no time for self-care, I was completely exhausted each night, and I was very angry with the extra effort I had to produce each day.

Honestly, I had to do something because I was completely burned out. I had developed anxiety and high blood pressure from my current job as I had been given a negative performance review. I knew what was coming next, so I took control of my own life and quit my job. Well, we all know the saying, "When one door closes, another one opens." There was nothing I wanted more than to do things on my own terms, have more time for myself, and make enough money without the job stress – this was my dream for living my empowered life. The problem was that at the time, I didn't know what I stood for. I didn't even have a voice. I was still traumatized from my negative work experience and all my past failures with network marketing were distracting me from moving forward in business.

I wanted to be able to fully and completely give all my love to my son by spending more time with him. I needed my husband to retire from his strenuous job, I had a passion to help other people do the same, and I wanted to have a career that would allow me to grow as a person while still being a loving mother and attentive, supportive wife to my husband. These were the goals of my dream life.

In the beginning, what I had in mind for my empowering people business was the complete opposite of how it all turned out. Yet, I am very grateful for what I have learned. I believed that all I needed was to implement SEO (also known as Search Engine Optimization – or giving my website the most exposure it could possibly receive) and my clients would just flock in for information. I thought to myself, "I can just sit behind a computer and write blogs that everyone from all over the world would come to visit. All I need to do is to coach people all day through the internet in my pajamas while getting paid." Besides, I just had to offer a freebie and the people would pour in, right? Well, that didn't happen at all. By then, I was running out of savings and my Employment Benefits were ending soon.

I realized I was not a "sit-behind-the-computer-and-grow-a-business" kind of professional. I needed to be in actual contact with my clients. Even though I did not like speaking in front of others, I did it. I felt that I was terrible at introducing myself at networking events, and that I had nothing to offer my audience. I found myself promoting fertility workshops and fertility coaching programs to grandmothers and old men: talk about depressing. I realized I had to do something about this.

After years of soul-searching, inner-healing, and trying to figure my life out, I appreciated that I had a lot to offer the world. People started to tell me just how powerful I was, but I still didn't understand it. I thought, "Me? Powerful?" I would ask myself, "You have such a long way to go. You have so much more work to do on yourself." However, I still didn't really know what I stood for in my life. I just knew I wanted to empower others, but I didn't know how?

I started to build my tool box of things that made me feel better, because I figured if they worked for me, they could work for others. I discovered Tapping (also known as EFT, which refers to emotional freedom technique, a method used to improve emotional health). I started working on tapping out all the negative energies that had been trapped inside of me. I started attending a lot of conferences and seminars, and it was at these events when I started to meet people just like myself who were experiencing similar life situations. They were entrepreneurs who wanted to give of their skills and talents to build their amazing businesses, and in connecting, I felt like I had come home. I became certified in NLP (neuro-linguistic programming), and learned the ability to shift negative energy using my mind and thoughts, as well as a Reiki Master, learning how to use my hands to build up and raise my vibration. I also enjoyed the power of working with a life coach and how much further I was able to proceed on my own life's journey. I started to embrace the teachings of well-known authors and teachers of holistic and new age theories. While practising sincere fasting and prayer, I wrote an e-book and created a program for women with infertility issues. Through all these new life applications, I started to gain strength and move forward to my ultimate vision and life-goals.

I learned how to connect with people, which lead me to cultivate a huge network of people. They were mostly mentors and people in similar circles with a common vision, who had experienced the same situations with similar interests as I had. Through my contacts and connections, I was able to start a radio show on Blog Talk called "The Life Coach Show" about connecting with life coaches and empowering an international audience.

By focusing on all the things that I loved in my life, and changing my attitude more positively, I now appreciate taking my son at the start of the school day and picking him up afterwards.

Through the trials of trying to figure it all out, I started two online coaching groups to help other coaches find their path. I started Niche Networkers and the second, The Core Group, a local social media group that provides resources and empowerment to others. With all this, I found that I really had a knack for leadership skills.

I had gone back to the drawing board so many times that I started to feel like the Saturday morning cartoon character who never really succeeded in catching his prey.

It was time to change my brand from Fertility Coach to Empowerment Coach. I still had a fertility piece to my brand, which made me satisfied, as it completed my repertoire of entrepreneurial skills. I had self-published an e-book called, *"Day 1: 101 Things to Consider on Day 1 of Your Cycle When You are Trying to Conceive."*

My vision is being fulfilled as I love working with my clients and helping them to find their own strengths, voices, and powers within themselves. I now brand myself as an Empowerment Awareness Coach and Consultant, Author, Speaker, and Reiki Master Instructor.

My goal is for people to really feel they can live their ideal lives through my empowerment awareness coaching, Reiki sessions, workshops, The Life Coach Radio Show, and marketing products.

My future is positive and bright as I have no intention of giving up. I see myself on stage and positively motivating a crowd of thousands. I am living my desires to the fullest, and I am empowering and healing others with my words. Looking back, it did not come easy. I had to work on making changes in my own life, and I had to fix it as I made mistakes, while learning from my life experiences. My goals for my company will be to house some of the most inspiring motivational and empowerment coaches and speakers. I cannot do it alone, and I will be leading a team of inspiring entrepreneurs with similar visions and the purpose of empowering the human race. My desire is to help people become aware of the power inside of them, helping them to find their voices that had been lost or taken away somewhere along their journeys. I am lessening the fears that have held them back from living their dreams of getting out into the world and making a difference, whether it's being a better parent, motivator, worker, healer, inventor, visionary, or just having a greater love for self. My company is about inspiring others to work on themselves and then to encourage them to go out and inspire the world.

Along with the right team, we will develop and assemble the right tools to help each individual live their empowered life. Together we can accomplish so much for the human race, and within my company, there will be a resource for everyone who needs support. This transformation won't be for everyone. But there will be support for those of you who want to heal and transform your lives.

My passion of finally having the flexibility to have work-life balance and spend quality time with my family is my motivation to finally say, "See, I never gave up, I kept trying and you can too." To all my friends and family who thought I would never succeed or that I should just get a job, I want to say, "Look at me now: I'm living my dreams and I'm making a difference in so many peoples' lives. For all the times when I didn't know how I was going to pay my bills, I say, "What bills?" My accountant takes cares of all our expenses." For all the times that I had a desire to help out a friend in need, and just didn't have the means, I say, "Here you go, my friend." And to all the people who made my journey challenging, I say, "Thank you; thank you for the challenge: it only made me stronger, because during my darkest times when my bank account was in the negative, and I cried myself to sleep, I knew

God heard my prayers and wiped away my tears. He stretched out his hands, picked me back up, and He gave me hope to keep going and a will to never quit."

Looking back at all of this, I'm grateful that my last paid job was the pits. I'm grateful that my husband was not able to be more helpful at times. If life was too cushy and smooth for me, I would not have pursued my dreams and passion.

When you have a bad day, you should look at it as a reminder of the work you need to do on yourself. Don't ignore the negative: find support and address it. Don't feel you need to live a life you're not happy with. Inside everyone is the power to make changes. Find your voice: YOU are responsible for you. Get out there in the world and make a difference. You don't have to be perfect. You can fix it as you go. Assemble your support team and get yourself empowered.

I'm so grateful for all of these experiences and what I have gained from them. I'm even grateful for all the nights when I would cry myself to sleep as I realized I only had God to rely on He was my only hope, and in my desperation to live my dream life, I learned over the months and years how to pray deep heartfelt prayers. I kept smiling, knowing that this is what I wanted for myself and eventually, I found a way to achieve my dreams, both personally and professionally. The bright side was that this is exactly what I wanted for myself, so I never gave up when something didn't work. Ultimately, things started to work for me. I know that if I can live my empowered life, you can too!

Dedicated to my Family, with love.

Andrea Lavallee is an Empowerment Awareness Consultant and Coach, is the founder of The Empowerment Coaching Group, and the host of the four time international radio show, The Life Coach Radio Show – connecting with Life Coaches and empowering the audience. She is a Reiki Master Instructor, Certified Life Coach, NLP Certified Practitioner, Author and Speaker. Andrea has a BA in Psychology and has been empowering people for over 15 years in the social services field before making to jump to Life Coaching and Reiki. Andrea is available for live speaking opportunities, in person workshops, and one on one coaching.

www.theempowermentcoachinggroup.com
https://www.facebook.com/empowermentcoachingbyandrea

VISION TIP   Vanessa Krichbaum

How I Lived My Peace

As a child, it was not part of the vision of my future to be a divorced, single parent. Like most little girls, I dreamed of being married, having children, and living in a happy home. In fact, after the death of my father when I was eight years old, there were times I fantasized that my Dad was still living, that he and my Mom were divorced, and that I simply spent time with him separately.

How ironic then, that I actually became one of those divorced parents, having to negotiate time, holidays, and events with my ex-husband. Our children were quite young when we became estranged and in the early days of our separation, the co-parenting was quite amicable. We still had family dinners and got together for Christmas and birthdays to celebrate. We even had summer vacation days together, which we all enjoyed.

This calm did not last. As we both moved on with our adult lives and made decisions independent of the other, more situations arose that caused dissention and conflict. We got caught in the divorced "I'm right, you're wrong" trap and usually under the guise of "this is best for the children." Believe me when I say, there is an entire system out there which profits from the collective conflict. Contentious divorce is a money and hate maker, taking much needed funds away from the parents and children.

During the height of our dissention, and the peak of my exhaustion, I refocused my thought energy on our hostilities stopping. I did not know how but there had to be a better way. And as I focused on peace between us, it slowly became a reality. We now agree to disagree because there are many correct answers and solutions to the same situation. More often than not, we can find common ground.

My epiphany in all of this was understanding; that directing negative feelings towards my ex-husband transcended to my children, at a cellular level. To feel hatred towards the father of my children was to tell my children that I loathed the part of him that lives in them. And that simply is not an option, as I love every piece of them. With this realization, I learned again to be grateful for the man who made these incredible children possible. I envisioned and created peace.

VISION TIP CONTRIBUTORS

Susan Lawrence

www.seedsofspirit.co.uk

Elizabeth Ann Pennington

eapennington@outlook.com

Angela T. Muskat

www.angelamuskat.com

Mélany Pilon

melanychat@hotmail.com

VISION TIPS CONTRIBUTORS

Melody Mbondiah

Melodymbondiah@outlook.com

Barbara Jasper

www.BarbaraJasper.com

Dvora Rotenberg

www.aspirelifecoaching.ca

Yonnette Kennedy

Yonnettekennedy@yahoo.com

VISION TIPS CONTRIBUTORS

Saskia Jennings-de Quaasteniet

www.creatingbeingwell.com

Vanessa Krichbaum

www.linkedin/in/vanessakrichbaum

CONCLUSION

Now that you have read each of these enlightening chapters and Vison Tips with the understanding what each of my co-authors have contributed to make this vision come to life, my hope is that you will feel an empowering and creative shift in your own world. Having a vision is a powerful direction for many things in this life.

My intention with this project was to inspire you to re-evaluate your life and how you may have allowed past experiences to affect the life you are living today. With so many perspectives revealed in this book, it would be a blessing to see how we can change the world with love, peace, and unity one soul at a time, beginning with your beautiful vision. I encourage you to stretch and let go of your own personal limitations as you continue to ponder the wisdom and life experiences of all my co-authors. They have openly allowed you into their world of emotions and various life experiences.

The value that is within this beautiful book is timeless. Just like gold never loses its value, the many perspectives of what love really is, has been tenderly poured into each chapter. This kind of wisdom is incalculable and worthy of review and application in one's daily life.

Now, my question to you is "Do you have a vision for a beautiful book of your very own? Do you want to inspire, motivate and encourage other? Do you feel you can help others to live a life without limiting beliefs? Have you gone through something that is incredible and know that others need to hear your story? I would be honored to guide and mentor you to compile and write a life changing anthology of your own. If you are a visionary that believes in yourself but just need the professional support and guidance to pull it all together. What are you waiting for? Contact me and let's discuss what your next steps would be to become one of LWL PUBLISHING HOUSE's newest VIP Compiler.

I have successfully managed, mentored, coached, and organized six groups of international co-authors and clients. That's approximately 150 published authors from around the world who are now recognized as leaders and experts among their peers. Or, if you would like to be a co-author, we have several ongoing anthology projects as well.

Now, I would love to help you create and manage your Best-Selling book project and create a "business out of a book" either as a co-author or VIP Compiler™.

As the Founder, CEO, and Publisher of LWL PUBLISHING HOUSE, I have supported and mentored other clients successfully and would love to help you become a Best Selling author as well.

I have learned through experience and my extensive training as a Level 3 Advanced Certified Life Coach, NLP Practitioner, Law of Attraction Wealth Practitioner and Registered Nurse how people cope effectively by having an organized system that brings balance with positive results! There really is a secret to helping others succeed just for you! I want to show you how as my VIP client.

I understand it's not always easy to keep things running smoothly, whether it relates to your business, personal goals and obligations while still building the life of your dreams. I understand the frustrations, tears, and stress. I want to assist you in making your dreams and goals a reality as a published author and I want to show you how to do it as quickly as possible as you live your life with a passion and purpose while earning a financial bonus just for bringing your book to life. Let's get started. Connect with me and let me mentor and coach you through from the beginning to publication.

Experience plus a passionate vision is a sure formula for success!"

Together we will develop a "Master Plan for your own success" and along the way eliminate any "Limiting Beliefs" that have been stopping you all this time. You may even be surprised at what you discover! Your passion is where your strength lies. My passion is all about bringing your passion to life without limitations!

To begin the exciting journey as a VIP Compiler™ with Anita on your own anthology book, or to learn more about becoming a co-author with LWL PUBLISHING HOUSE in one of our many anthologies, please visit our Facebook page "LWL PUBLISHING HOUSE", visit our website: www.lwlpublishinghouse.com, or email: lwlclienthelp@gmail.com.

Anita Sechesky,

Founder and CEO of Anita Sechesky - Living Without Limitations Inc., Founder and Publisher of LWL PUBLISHING HOUSE, Registered Nurse, Certified Professional Coach, NLP and LOA Wealth Practitioner, Best-Seller Consultant, multiple International Best-Selling Author, Workshop Facilitator, Keynote Speaker, Trainer, and Conference Host.

To Ardith,

Always remember to
Go-For-It!

CMerodis
Mar 18, 2016

CPSIA information can be obtained
at www.ICGtesting.com
Printed in the USA
LVOW04s1010160116

470437LV00007B/26/P

9 780993 964831